Unstoppable Attitude

Unstoppable Attitude

The Principles, Practices,
Patterns & Psychology for
Achieving Your Highest Goals and
Living the Fulfilling Life you
Have Always Dreamed Of

Duane Marino

Prominent Books

Writing: Duane Marino
Editing & Layout: Writer Services, LLC

ISBN 10: 1-942389-10-8
ISBN 13: 978-1-942389-10-1

Prominent Books and the Prominent Books logo are Trademarks of Prominent Books, LLC

Table of Contents

Introduction

People often ask me how I maintain such a positive outlook, which I find odd, because I do not consider myself to be especially optimistic, at least not in the way most define it. Instead, I've conditioned myself to be a realist, meaning I try to see my life as objectively as possible, without making it better or worse than it really is. I imagine tomorrow being better than today because I know I possess the discipline, drive, desire and dedication to use any tool I can find to improve it.

I also don't consider myself to be a pump-up motivator for other people. If some people find me motivating, it's because I provide inspirational education or specific strategies that will improve someone's outcome and that's why I call myself a strategist.

Sometimes life comes at us in unpredictable and unkind ways, and though I condition myself on a daily basis to have an Unstoppable Attitude, I will admit to being far from perfect and do have a bad day now and then. The important thing is the speed with which I bounce back, without letting those low points gain momentum. We can't control all the cards we are dealt but we can control how we interpret the cards and how we choose to play our hand.

Recently it dawned on me that my interest in motivation and personal development started when I was about ten years old. My mother gave me a large, awkwardly bound brown book called *Guidewords*. I put it beside my bed and

1

read a random quote or passage every day for years. I've often wondered if the seeds planted from that book during my younger years germinated and grew into some of my interests later in life. I've also given much thought as to why my mother—a wonderful woman but with whom I often had a challenging relationship—gave me such an inspirational book. This irony taught me that people come into your life for a reason, and my mother gave me the gift of an Unstoppable Attitude, both figuratively and literally. The saying that "steel hardens steel" definitely holds true here.

Let me assure you that anyone with an Unstoppable Attitude maintains it deliberately. They may not have had formal training, but whether they realize it or not they are employing methodologies and/or philosophies that keep their mindset in check. Just like physical hygiene, mental hygiene requires regular effort and real work.

The nature and difficulty of this work depends on a number of things, such as family history and personality type. For example, although I love people and can be very social, I am an introvert at heart; this means I prefer to recharge my batteries and try to cope with things alone. For several years, whenever an obstacle popped up in my life (and believe me, there were many not of my own doing, and outside my control) I would try to handle it all by myself. By age twenty-three things became overwhelming and I began to develop a very bad attitude, to put it mildly. (As I chose to divorce my limiting personal story years ago, I will spare you all the details; however, if you're curious, feel free to take a peek at the last few chapters of *Unstoppable Selling*. It will give you some insight into what I was going through and what drove me to choose this career).

Unstoppable Attitude probably should have preceded my first book—the Amazon Best Seller *The Six Sales Powers to Unstoppable Selling*—and my second—*Unstoppable Money*—because your attitude really is everything. My intent for this book is to give you access to the same tools I use, and continue to use, on myself and with my clients. It covers a lot of ground and some suggestions may seem outlandish or even silly, but I promise you, when used with focused attention and positive intention, they will systematically tear you down and rebuild you, for the better, from the inside out. Together, over time, these strategies provide a deep and wide multi-pronged approach that would make even the most closed-minded therapist and resistant client have dozens of "aha!" moments.

From early childhood we are taught about the importance of physical hygiene. We must bathe, brush our teeth and put on clean clothes each day or we will stick out like a sore thumb and even be shunned. But very few of us are taught how to "brush" our brains!

Reader, let's say that on average we're awake for fifteen hours a day. If we have one hundred random thoughts per hour, that's fifteen hundred random thoughts a day. I would argue that for most people, the majority of these thoughts involve some form of negativity—things like: "Why do I work here?; She's terrible!; He's awful!; They can't drive; Who taught you to park?!; I'm too short; I'm too tall; I will never master this; I don't have enough money" and on and on.

With so many negative thoughts floating around you would think we'd be taught how to clean up our minds, just as we use a virus scanner to seek out and eliminate possible threats to our computer systems. Think of this book as your personal virus scanner, helping you detect and get rid of threats to your mental well-being. It will also give you the tools needed to identify someone else with an unkempt mind. There is an unlimited number of ways in which our attitudes can become contaminated and just like a computer with a virus we can start to experience operational inefficiencies and a loss of effectiveness. I think the biggest problem with the "feel good movement" of the past few decades is that people think they shouldn't have any problems! And let's face it, many of our problems are really "first world problems" as many of us like to say these days.

That said, we all have things we want or need to work on, so this book should NOT be read like any ordinary book, but like an owner's manual for your mind. I suggest you read no more than one chapter per day and ideally condition yourself with each concept for a week before moving on the next. Contemplate, meditate, cultivate and analyze each page and apply what you are learning. The tools in this book, when practiced, will produce profound and real shifts in your life. How do I know? Because I am always my first guinea pig. I humbly "walk the talk" with each and every thing that I teach and then share what I learn with tens of thousands of people, who in turn share their results with me!

I am going to make a bold promise: this book will give you many new tools, perspectives, re-frames and ways to approach life's challenges and choices that, if used as directed, will transform how you act and react to almost everything you do! Many of these tools are rooted in personal development technologies for which I am certified.

They are rather complex, so for our purposes here I provide a brief introduction with the understanding that you will continue researching the things that will most assist you in cultivating your Unstoppable Attitude. And remember, repetition is the mother of skill, so condition yourself by re-visiting these strategies frequently! Some chapters are meant to purposely provoke, prod and stir you up. You will find some concepts are interventionist in nature and only need to be reviewed once, while others are practices that are best done on a regular—even daily basis.

Two fundamental principles I live by is that every aspect of our personal and professional lives (and the results we get) are due to either the **information** we have or the **execution** of that information. So, in simple terms, any time we want to make a change, even to our attitudes, we need to step back and assess our information and our execution. Every chapter in this book is based on those two fundamental points.

PLEASE approach this book with a playful, open-minded and yet skeptical attitude. Be sure to keep your fear and ego on the shelf so that you can ascertain the validity of the concepts and exercises. At the same time, I hope that you will consider my suggestions about how to use the strategies to cultivate an Unstoppable Attitude, avoid slipping backwards and deepen your appreciation, understanding and application of their benefits.

I hope you enjoy and apply *Unstoppable Attitude*! Feel free to contact me through our website, Facebook, LinkedIn, YouTube, Instagram, Twitter or any other social media outlet you can find me on. Ask me questions, start a dialogue or tell me your success stories.

Now, enough of the introduction. Head down, horns out and straight ahead. Let's do this!

The Magic Number: 86,400

How many people say that they can't go to the gym, can't take on that new role at work or can't make more contacts, merely because they don't have the time? My friends, you're never going to get more time; it is a constraint and a measured absolute. You can however, learn to bend time. What's the saying? Time flies when you're having fun. When you improve your attitude about anything you change your perception of time with regard to it and our perception is our reality. Let's face it, there may not always be equal employment opportunities due to age, size, sex, race, education, limited access to people or social restrictions, but everyone has an equal opportunity employer and her name is "TIME".

Everyone, regardless of their circumstances has 86,400 seconds in a day, 1440 minutes in a day, 24 hours in a day, 7 days a week, 52 weeks a year, 365 days a year and 10 years in a decade. When you drive your car, where you drove and what you can see in the rear view mirror (your past) isn't nearly as important as where you are headed and what you see in the front windshield (your present and future). You are given 86,400 time credits every single day, to use in any way you wish. Invest them or waste them, every hour, every minute, every second is a new choice point. The last minute or last hour doesn't really matter. I ask you, how do you intend on spending your next 86,400 choices? Time management is not about getting more time, as that is impossible, but about making different decisions with the time you've got.

Since the age of twenty-five I've been traveling an average of five days a week and at one point I had a client in Ohio to whom I would drive six hours every other month. One blustery and snowy winter night, I had just returned home from another Ohio trip. It was around nine o'clock and I had just about an hour to grab a bite to eat and a short nap before I had to leave again for a workshop in Ottawa starting at eight the next morning. Faced with at least another six-hour drive in brutal winter weather, I was completely stressed out. As I hurried toward the front door, I saw my ten-year-old daughter waiting for me there.

She gave me a solemn look. "Do you have to leave again, Papa?"

I looked down at her, shook off my guilt and said, "We don't have to do anything. We *get* to."

I was building my business from scratch and could not believe that people in Ohio and Ottawa were actually demanding to see me. I also realized that it was all by my own choice. You don't "got" to do anything either, you "get" to. I believe there will come a day when we will all look back and wish we were still doing some of the things we do begrudgingly today, so why not enjoy them now? Think about it, if you can't enjoy what you are doing right now, what makes you think you will enjoy it any differently in the future? How you spend your time is a choice and that choice starts NOW.

There are many important dates in our lives, but arguably the two most important are those that appear on our tombstone: the day we are born and the day we die. However, most of us give little thought to the dash in between. This small, seemingly insignificant symbol represents all the choices we've made during the time we have on earth, however long that is. Ask yourself, how are you spending your dash? How are you going to spend your next 86,400 choices? Where, on what and to whom are you giving your focus and energy? Your energy flows where your focus goes. You can't manage time; all you can manage is your thoughts, emotions, focus, choices and actions in the time you have.

Exercise: Write the word "dash" somewhere to remind you of this concept, and look at it daily for one week.

This may sound strange, but I am inspired by going to cemeteries as it reminds me of my limited time here. As I walk among the rows of graves, knowing one day mine will be among them, I always imagine all of the blood, sweat, tears, love, frustration, joy, trials and tribulations these people faced during their dashes. And I imagine that if they could speak to me they would shout, "Now is your time to live, forgive, love, help and enjoy your life!"

Here's a perspective changer: change the words "got to" to "get to"! Forgive my poor grammar, but we don't "got to" go to work, have a shower, raise our children, exercise, pay bills or wash the car, we "get to"! A small shift from "got to" to "get to" can bring a real sense of appreciation and gratitude to everything you do!

"To live in hearts we leave behind, is not to die."

—Tom Campbell
NASA Physicist and Consciousness Explorer

The Eight Universal Causes of Failure

Something to think about: personal development became big business in the 20th century, but its roots go back millennia; in fact, there is a 2500-year-old philosophy that suggests it is easier to avoid failure than it is to seek success. I believe we were all born to be great at something, so rather than seeking success, maybe try to avoid the causes of failure.

Exercise: Think of a goal you would like to achieve. Then, for each area below assign a number from 1 to 10 that represents an honest assessment of yourself (you may need an objective, honest person to help evaluate you):

The first cause of failure is bad intentions. If you don't feel good about what you are doing it will eventually weigh on you and cause you to dial it down, burn out or quit. Others won't fully support you because they sense your incongruent approach to your own goal.

My intentions for this goal are very positive.   _____/10?

The second cause of failure is incorrect views. This essentially means you are either lacking information or are studying the wrong stuff.

My views regarding this goal are correct.   _____/10?

The third cause of failure is ineffective speech. Talking to yourself or others in an ineffective or negative way will not help your cause.

My speech is always effective and aligned with my goal.   ____/10?

The fourth cause of failure is not being in the right livelihood. Perhaps your current livelihood is not aligned with who you are, or worse yet, is harmful to yourself or others in some way.

I'm in an appropriate livelihood that supports my goal and helps other people in some way.   ____/10?

The fifth cause of failure is taking the wrong actions. You either don't know what to do or choose to do the wrong things.

My consistent actions are in alignment with my goal.   ____/10?

The sixth cause of failure is low self-awareness. Low self-awareness makes it very difficult to evaluate, improve or avoid any of the other causes of failure.

My self-awareness is accurate in relation to this goal.   ____/10?

The seventh cause of failure is lack of concentration. Some tasks and achievements take hours, days, weeks, months or even years of continual concentration to break open.

My power of concentration is fully applied towards my goal.   ____/10?

The eighth cause of failure is lack of effort. Frequency and intensity of effort, day in and day out, is where the rubber meets the road.

My effort is appropriate to what is needed
to hit my goal.   ____/10?

As you will see later on in this book, I "meditate" on these eight causes in relation to all my goals, every single day.

"Identify your problems, but give your power and energy to solutions."

—Tony Robbins
Entrepreneur, Philanthropist & Coach

Analysis to the Point of Paralysis

Ever wonder how a cell phone really works? What the mechanics are behind that amazing little mobile computer we talk into once in a while when we feel like it? I get off a plane and it automatically locates me, changes time zones and forwards my calls. I have some knowledge about GPS, satellites, triangulation and electronics, but I could not get into specific detail on how a cell phone actually operates. All I really care about is that it works. This applies to many things in our lives, we don't always need to know how something works, sometimes we just need to be grateful that it does. I re-write my Goals and Gratitudes every six months and briefly review them every day. How does this brief activity keep me positively motivated and help bring resources into my life that can help me achieve what I desire? Who cares, I'm just grateful that it does! I entered into this daily exercise with open-minded skepticism on September 13, 2001 (yes, there is a story about that), and have witnessed and experienced its benefits in a real and major way ever since.

Needing to know "how" or "why" everything works before you engage in it can waste a lot of time. These types of questions can lead to a negative mindset that creates unresolvable and unrelated answers, similar to asking "Why me?" when something doesn't work. Think of "Why me?" and "How so?" as classes you should never attend. Instead, notice when something does work, for you or someone else, then use it over and over and over. When it isn't working, try something else. In business and in life it is sometimes enough to just model or copy what works without over-analyzing the *how*. Down the road, it might be fun to try to determine the why, but for now just use the tools. You don't need to know everybody at the tool factory or how a hammer is built to start hammering nails.

Too much thinking and analysis can lead to inaction and paralysis.

Much time has been spent trying to figure out what makes a successful person, but the reality is that a good portion of success is simply showing up, ready to play, every day. Most successful people are the ones left standing after everyone else gave up. There is a lot to be said about dumbing it down, keeping it simple and working hard every single day.

"The ultimate authority must always rest with the individual's own reason, critical analysis and knowing when and how to apply their knowledge."

—The Dalai Lama

Beliefs

Many of our most persistent, pervasive and permanent problems stem from our beliefs. The process of how we create beliefs about ourselves and the world around us is fascinating. Our opinions, beliefs and convictions are created and supported by our imagination, information and experiences. And because our imagination, information and experiences are subjective, we will all interpret things differently and therefore have different beliefs. You may believe you're a great person, a terrible business person, a great parent or a poor one. It doesn't matter whether our beliefs are true or false, good or bad, right or wrong; what matters is that they are filters through which we see the world and ourselves and they can either empower or disempower us and other people.

Our beliefs can be restrictive so that they block off many new experiences, new information and even the use of our imagination. This skeptical mindset can really limit us, keep us from improving and even steal the juice from life. Conversely, our filters can be so loose and open that we never develop a set of beliefs pertaining to who we are or the world around us. Being this open-minded is usually a plus, but when taken to this extreme it could lead to all sorts of other issues. The key here is to have an open mind and a healthy skepticism. Remember, the mark of an effective mind is the ability to entertain any thought without judging it.

Beliefs come in varying degrees of strength, and they affect us in different ways. Pliable, soft beliefs are just opinions. Very strong beliefs are convictions. If you have an opinion that you are good at your career, the way in which you approach it will be completely different than if you have a conviction that you are good at it. I have witnessed individuals who believe in themselves so fiercely (even before acquiring a real skill set), that they become great in spite of their initial lack of skills.

That said, having strong beliefs does pose some dangers, most notably belief traps and belief edits.

Let's say you believe you can make $15,000 a month. Doesn't this also mean you do NOT believe you can make $25,000? This is a perfect example of a belief trap. Beliefs that once served you can later trap you. A better (untrapped) belief would be, "I know I can improve my income, so for now I will move towards changing myself in whatever ways I have to until I hit $15,000 a month. Once I get there, I will reassess."

Belief edits are evident when, out of a need for certainty, you start ignoring and discounting anything and everything that goes against your beliefs. When feeling certain, we release the happy hormones, endorphins; when feeling uncertain we release the unhappy hormone, cortisol. This means that unless we are vigilant, we are hormonally wired to avoid or resist anything that creates uncertainty and contradicts our current belief systems. To see this in action, start talking to someone about something that completely contradicts something they believe in, then watch their eyes glaze over as they delete or edit your words. For more information on this, I suggest researching the term "The Certainty Bias."

Exercise: Get yourself into different environments, put yourself in front of people you normally avoid, read things you have never or would never normally think of reading, visit websites that contradict your opinions, eat foods you have never eaten and go to social events you have never attended. Expanding your comfort zones is an important part of tearing down your unsupportive beliefs, as well as helping you to have compassion, tolerance, patience and wisdom for those different from you.

Blinders

A racehorse wears leather blinders that restrict it from looking off to the left or to off to the right. It can only look straight ahead. The horse is also assisted by an ultra-light-weight jockey who holds the reins firm to make sure it doesn't turn its head and become distracted. Although one was bred for power and speed and the other is selected for their diminutive size and weight, the two work in concert to reach the finish line as quickly as possible and they do so with limited vision and strict focus.

As my friend Joe Girard (the Guinness World Record #1 Salesperson in History) taught me, sometimes this is all it takes to be super successful. Have one unwavering purpose and just keep improving, growing and showing up until you get what you want, never getting distracted and keeping your eyes on the prize!

Exercise: For one week, simply identify what your unproductive distractions are.

Blueprints

We all have a picture in our minds of what our lives should be like. This "blueprint" may have developed early in life through our families, teachers, friends, enemies, television shows we watch, music we listen to and stories we read. They also may come to us suddenly or over time.

As we go through life with this internal blueprint in mind, we naturally feel fulfilled when our life conditions match what we expect our life to be and frustrated when they don't. Obviously, the bigger the difference between our expectations and conditions, the more intense our negative feelings.

When you find yourself unhappy with your life you have three choices: change your expectations (blueprint), change your conditions (life) or a little bit of both (probably the most practical and common solution).

Ironically, it's also common that once we start to feel fulfilled and satisfied, we may start to engage in self-sabotaging behaviors, creating gaps and differences once again between what we want and how our life is. It's almost as if the struggle is more comfortable than the arrival. Or perhaps we spend so much time, effort and money trying to achieve that the achievement itself, once reached, is anti-climatic as it relaxes our nervous systems to such an extent that we unconsciously create drama and circumstances that will put us back under pressure and discomfort, where we have been more used to living.

Self-sabotage can destroy progress in any area of your life; however, when properly understood this "addiction to pressure" can be very powerful and productive. For instance, when I became completely debt-free at the age of thirty-four, I started buying investment properties, not just for the obvious investment value, but because I recognized the elimination of financial pressure was making me lazy.

Climbing a mountain is different from staying on the peak and it requires a different blueprint. That's why as you get close to achieving your goal it's crucial to blueprint a whole new bunch of expectations of how you want things to be once you reach the top of that mountain. That way, you'll pressure yourself to stay on top of your game while you strive for other peaks rather than relaxing at the top for too long or start sliding back down after you've reached your goal.

Exercise: Write down the words "Relationships", "Work" and "Self" on three separate sheets of paper and draw a circle around them in the size and proportion as to how you rank them in importance in your life (most important is the biggest, the least important is the smallest). Then, for each area, list what you want to move towards and what you want to move away from. This exercise will increase your clarity of what your blueprint is now and what you would like it to become, in these three crucial areas.

Dominant Thoughts

Self-awareness is the beginning of self-improvement.

Years ago, while having trouble focusing I took a piece of paper and wrote the words "Dominant Thoughts" on it then placed it on my desk. Any time my eyes looked at it, I made myself do a "thought audit" and I wrote down what I was thinking about. The results were truly bizarre, enlightening and often laughable.

Whatever you give your thoughts and energy to expands. If your thoughts are negative or scattered, it will be harder to get anything positive or productive accomplished. Thoughts that you impress on your mind regularly will be expressed in your life and business automatically. Change your thoughts and you change your life.

If you want to know why your life is the way it is today, analyze your thoughts from yesterday.

So what are your dominant thoughts?

Exercise: Write "Dominant Thoughts" on a piece of paper and place it somewhere your eyes will notice it throughout the day. Every time you look at it, ask yourself, "What are my dominant thoughts right now?" and write down what you find. You will find your answers interesting to say the least.

Kill the ANTs and Shut Down Your Collectives

At one time or another, we have all fallen victim to an ANT (Automatic Negative Thought) infestation. I used to have so many ANTs, that my wild and untrained mind was like a "Drunk Monkey" that uncontrollably and randomly moved from one weak branch to another, creating havoc for myself and anyone that got in the way.

Typical ANTs may include, "Why do I work here? I'm not good enough. I'm too fat. I hate her. Why would someone say that to me? Why do I get all the bad customers? This will never work." When you have random ANTs triggered by certain internal or external cues, you are trapped in what I call a "Collective".

A Collective is a reactive thought accompanied by a chain of physiological responses that occurs when we are exposed to some stimuli that we associate with danger, negativity, ego or fear. Collectives are not in and of themselves a bad thing; in fact, they are supposed to help us survive. For example, if a goldfish is enjoying a swim in a warm stream and is almost eaten by a large green fish with sharp teeth, it may then associate fear and anxiety with warm water, sharp teeth or even that specific shade of green. Subsequent exposure to these things will then trigger its fight, flight or freeze response. This response is hardwired into the brain and is an excellent tool for avoiding repetitive threats. Goldfish aren't the only ones who install Collectives; in fact, it is a defense mechanism all sentient beings use. When we encounter something dangerous, embarrassing, hurtful or negative we might subconsciously associate the objects around that experience with the event, thus creating Collectives designed to help us avoid those same objects later on.

The problem is, Collectives do not distinguish between a genuine threat to our survival and low-level stressors. In our complex world, we are constantly surrounded by thousands of stressors that could result in our creating Collectives around some relatively harmless environments and objects. For instance, you may find you experience sudden anxiety around certain colors, or when you hear a particular voice or when you need to make some phone calls. These might have been caused by just one bad experience earlier in your life when some of those things happened to be present and your brain linked a threat to them. It's illogical but very real and Collectives can create all sorts of problems for us in our daily lives. So when a stimulus occurs that we link to a Collective it will trigger our subconscious minds to fire off a reaction. And because emotion travels much faster than conscious thought, like a runaway train, our rational minds and physical responses get hijacked and we can start to behave in all sorts of crazy ways.

How can we shut down inappropriate Collectives?

Exercise: Collectives can be rendered neutral simply by realizing, with your fully conscious analytical mind, when and where this link was installed. How can you identify the time of installation of a negative Collective?

1. Identify a situation, object or person that creates an involuntary negative response that seems disproportionate or even extreme based on the actual event or stimulus (I'm not proud of this, but I used to scream like a child whenever I saw a spider. I even jumped on chairs a few times!).

2. Sit quietly with your eyes closed and do a timeline regression, looking further and further back at your life. Take one year at a time, asking yourself, "Did I have this issue at that age?" until you feel like you have found the year it was installed. Then, review that year slowly and all the typical situations you were in, until you have an "aha!" moment and have located the event that installed the issue. (If you go all the way back to birth and can't find the event, contact me for help).

3. You will know you have found the source that created the Collective when you find yourself giggling incredulously at the memory of it (when I found my source memory that installed my spider phobia I was both astonished and entertained).

4. Test your discovery by introducing the stimulus and noting if your reaction has lessened or—hopefully—disappeared. I don't keep spiders as pets but am no longer frozen by their appearance and if I ever feel anxious about them again, I simply refer back to my source memory and the fear instantly dissipates.

How can we Kill the ANTs?

If you're like many people, you have probably tried to rid yourself of automatic negative thoughts through sheer will, only to be frustrated when they remain or are even magnified. If I say to you, "Don't think about a purple onion," what do you think about? Exactly—a purple onion! The good news is that ANTs can be done away with by using this simple, three-part process: SPOT, STOP and SQUASH.

SPOT: Start by becoming acutely aware of your emotional and physical state and what triggers negative reactions. For example, perhaps when you see a certain person you react with feelings of anxiety, anger or uneasiness. Such feelings are experienced through changes in your pulse, breathing, perspiration, location of muscle tension, uneasiness in your stomach, et cetera. This negative association is known as a *negative anchor* and once you spot it, you are in a position to collapse it. In fact, just becoming aware of the negative association occasionally causes laughter, which is a telltale sign you have found the source of your negative feelings and may even resolve the issue right then and there.

If spotting it doesn't weaken or kill the ANT, you must STOP it by disrupting your pattern. You can do this by driving the image of a red stop sign into your internal visual awareness every time you spot the ANT. While holding onto the image of the STOP sign, you may find taking a deep breath and leaning back an inch can also assist in breaking your pattern. It may take weeks to condition a pattern interrupt for permanent results, but this process will work.

If after spotting and stopping, the ANT persists, it is time to SQUASH it. This requires a dramatic, even bizarre physical action at the onset of the ANT-induced anxiety. For example, you might contort your body into an odd position, create a goofy hand gesture or facial expression, do jump squats or make strange sounds. This disruption in your physiology will SQUASH the negative associations by interrupting and confusing the habitual runaway-train physiological patterns that fire inside of you.

Exercise: Train yourself to SPOT your ANTs, then STOP them by disrupting your internal patterns through creating an internal image of a massive stop sign when the ANT is triggered. If needed, SQUASH the ANT through a sudden radical and odd shift in your physiology.

There is no way to completely avoid installing ANTs and Collectives in your future; they are a natural reaction to our environment and life circumstances. But believe me, you can kill any harmful or unproductive ANT and collapse any Collective using these steps. In fact, I have found that just being aware of these phenomena helps to reduce the frequency and intensity of installing any new patterns, as well as lessening the negative impact of ones you may already have.

Fear and Ego

Fear and ego are in my opinion the two main obstacles to our growth. Like ANTS and Collectives, they are there to protect us, but when they are given free, unobserved rein over our lives, fear and ego can become invisible fences keeping us from authentic connection with others, taking on new challenges and considering alternate viewpoints. When we always need to be right or don't try things because of fear, we cut ourselves off from new knowledge, people and opportunities. To have an Unstoppable Attitude, it is imperative that you check your fear and ego at the door each day.

Exercise: Do a daily review of your intentions, thoughts, actions, where you went, what you did, what you didn't do, who you would and wouldn't interact with, and the quantity and quality of those interactions. Then, tell yourself that next time you won't be held back by the fetters of fear and the illusion of ego.

Nicknames

I love nicknames. A good nickname can really sum up how you feel, or want to feel about someone or something. It can make a difficult person bearable and a likeable person loveable, so choose them thoughtfully and responsibly.

The next time you want to change an outcome in your life or someone else's, consider giving them, or yourself, a creative, fun and appropriate nickname. You'll find it instantly reframes your feelings toward the person or situation.

Exercise: Give three people a nickname that reframes how you would like to start feeling toward them. Give a few negative past events nicknames that will change how you feel about it. Give some positive past events nicknames that will increase your positive feelings toward those. Give some upcoming future events nicknames that make you feel differently about their arrival. I'm laughing to myself as I write this, reflecting on all the silly nicknames I have given so many good and bad people, places, events and things … hilarious!

Fine-Tune Your BS Meter

Reader, I believe we are all born with the ability to tell when someone is fibbing, exaggerating, saying something that may not work or generally giving us a hard time through false information. That said, some of us are more in tune with our BS Meter than others.

This may sound odd, but truth generally feels light in your body, while a falsehood will feel heavy. There is even a science called "applied kinesiology" that utilizes muscle testing in much the same way. Consider researching it if you wish to fine-tune your BS Meter.

Exercise: Listen to conversations, watch some controversial YouTube videos, so-called "Real News" and "Fake News" and observe others, trying to get a sense of what they are saying as feeling "light" (true) or "heavy" (false).

Take Your Child to Work Day

Every year, companies in North America and several other regions around the world take part in "Take Your Child To Work Day". It's an opportunity for your son or daughter to watch how you act and react while at work and learn to model themselves after you. If you had the opportunity to bring your child to work with you, would you want to? I do it all the time.

Now, let's take it one step further. Pretend your child will be shadowing you from the moment you wake up in the morning until you go to bed at night. What would you want him or her to witness in terms of your lifestyle, work ethic, processes, attitude, skills, habits, relationships, ethics, drive, et cetera? Would you want your child to be exposed to your every thought and behavior regarding your work? What do you think or say when you see certain people at work, when you have an upset customer? Would you be able to verbalize such thoughts to your child? It puts things in a new perspective, doesn't it?

Exercise: As you are in the busy-ness of your business, keep the concept of "Bring Your Child to Work Day" in your mind and make any changes accordingly. If you don't have children, imagine that some impressionable young person you care about is there, hanging on your every word and action.

Self-Help

At the age of twenty-five and feeling personally and professionally lost, I embarked on a search for answers that resulted in a major career change as well as a lot of travel. While on a business trip to Kingston, Ontario I went to a bookstore, stumbled into the self-help section and picked up the first book that caught my eye. It was Tony Robbins' "Awaken the Giant Within," and after reading a few random pages I was convinced it had been written for me. Within a week I had finished that sizable book and realized it was the first one I'd ever read from cover to cover. Until then, I was never interested in the things I was studying.

When learning—or trying to learn—in school, I would always ask myself, "When will I ever use this?" (My answer was usually never). As a result, I would often zone out and when I did listen, it was only with enough effort to pass the test. I did not deeply absorb the teachings or commit them to long-term memory. There are undoubtedly many students who disengage from their "education" in this manner.

But Tony Robbins' book was different because I could see how I could and would use every single page. In fact, at that time I needed that information very badly. This experience showed me that when the right message and messenger appear, magic can happen, and it was a lesson I've never forgotten. That's why as a strategist, coach, consultant and trainer, I only focus on concepts my clients would be able to use every day. I also focus on developing sales processes, coaching sales people and building athletes because those are the areas in which I have the most experience, success and consistent exposure to. But I also realize, not everyone is ready for the message.

When you are truly motivated, desperate, driven, hungry or faced with the realization that some part of you is needing a change or perhaps even dying, it is an opportunity to catapult you onto another path.

I am living proof of how much we can change. Since picking up that book all those years ago, I have taken speed-reading courses so I could read faster and retain more; authored three books, created about 100,000 pages of written and online content and 4000 training videos. This, from a guy who had never read a book before he was twenty-five! If I had to guess, I'd say I've now read close to 500 books on the arts of fulfillment and the sciences of achievement, attended fifty workshops, spent about 20,000 hours doing online research and more time and money than I want to think about on post- University self-education workshops.

Desperation and passion can be potent motivators and educators. It is very hard to excel at something you don't love, but you can also fall in love with something you find you are good at. And since anything worth having is worth studying, decide what you want to have and become obsessed with your self-education. I'd be willing to bet that whatever you want in life, someone has written a book on it, built a website around it, recorded a video about it or created a workshop showing you how to get it. Become obsessed with learning more and earning more!

Circles of Focus

In my timeline I seem to recall that Forrest Gump said, "Life IS like a box of chocolates" (or at least that's how I remember it, but according to the Mandela Effect he apparently said "Life WAS like a box of chocolates." Go check that out for yourself).

In any event, I think life is like a donut.

Picture a small circle within a larger circle—we'll call them our "circles of focus". The outer circle is what I call our "circle of worry" and contains things we can worry about but not control, such as most things on the news, the weather, the economy, natural disasters around the world, politics, et cetera. Essentially, anything and everything besides yourself. Focusing on things you can worry about but not control is a source of distress and elevates the stress hormones insulin and cortisol (and suppresses all the good hormones such as endorphins, testosterone, progesterone and estrogen), which triggers the states of fight, flight or freeze. Prolonged exposure to this unease and "dis-ease" leads to the increased probability of disease of almost every kind.

When distressed, train yourself to immediately ask, "Can I control this?" or "What aspects of this can I control?" Then choose to work only on what you can control, period. Pointless worry is unhealthy and unproductive.

If we do not change our focus, we will overlook the other circle, which contains everything we may worry about but can control. This would be anything to do with us: how we treat others, our skills, attitudes, gratitudes, goals, the meaning we choose to attach to events, our body language, our interactions, our business practices, et cetera. The truth is, there are many factors we can control in almost every situation, but they will go unnoticed if we focus on our circle of worry. Think of it this way, even if you were in solitary confinement, you could control what you chose to think about, which would change your entire experience and interpretation of it.

Like any muscle, as you get better at continually shifting your focus onto what you can control, you will begin to worry less about what you can't control. Your fears will slip away.

There is a saying that FEAR stands for False Evidence Appearing Real. What we fear rarely if ever comes to pass in the way we fear it. And fear is the ugly step child of worry; it's hard to have one without the other. Practice the discipline of dividing your circle of worry from your circle of control, and you will realize that you can control the most important aspects of your life and finally give up all that unhealthy worry altogether.

To make it even simpler, there are only two primary human emotions: fear and love. By focusing on what you can control you will expand all the emotions that can spring from that sort of positive vibration, and by not giving energy to what you can't control you will diminish all of those negatively associated emotions as well.

Exercise: Draw a "donut" and write the word "Control" in the center. On the outside dough of the donut, write the words "Worry/Can't Control", and keep it nearby throughout the day. Whenever something is causing you distress, immediately categorize it and write it down in one of the circles. This clarity will help you make better choices.

"A coward dies a thousand times before his death, but the valiant taste death but once. It seems to me most strange that we should fear, as what will come, will come, when and how it chooses."

—William Shakespeare

Dis-ease

What exactly does it mean to be in the "flu season"? Does the weather radar show germs flying into your city like migrating geese? Those germs were there last month, and the month before that. It is no coincidence that flu season coincides with our distress season, when we tend to be faced with financial pressures, holiday travel and inclement, erratic weather, struggling to finish the same amount of work with less working days and forced to be around people we may not like. These things, and others like them, all reduce our ease.

Stress is neutral and when used properly can be helpful in making daily decisions and taking action. I mentioned earlier that I use the stress of investment property ("good debt") and goal setting to motivate me. As already mentioned, this in turn releases the hormones insulin and cortisol, making us feel heavy and anxious; it also causes all sorts of other problems like gaining fat, suppression of testosterone, progesterone, endorphins and estrogen, depressed immune systems, and loss of energy and focus. On the other hand, when you feel like you're winning, you move into eustress—or "good stress"—which causes beneficial psychological and physiological reactions. I find goal setting increases my continual feeling of winning.

Start paying close attention to what causes distress and disease in your life, and use some of the tools in this book to reduce and eliminate them. Many of the same tools, when applied in a slightly different manner, can actually increase your eustress and give you a natural high. Your mind drives the most powerful and natural pharmacology available anywhere—your endocrine and hormonal systems—so study them and then use them wisely.

Avoid "CNN"—
Constantly Negative News

(Note: This is in no way meant as a derogatory remark toward the media outlet that uses the same acronym.)

Exercise: Go and buy a newspaper, take a red pen and circle all the articles that make you feel bad, and then take a green pen to circle all the articles that perk you up. You will likely discover, as I have, that if your goal is to have an Unstoppable Attitude, you may want to avoid this kind of "bad news" entirely.

When I'm traveling, it is not unusual for the hotel staff to thoughtfully place a newspaper outside my door in the morning. When I open my door and see it lying there, I instinctively look away and step over it so I don't catch the mind viruses inside. When housekeeping cleans my room, they usually bring the paper inside and, again, ever so thoughtfully place it on a table, probably thinking I missed it. When I see it there, I immediately put it in the recycling box.

Did you know that ALL of the mainstream media in North America is owned by only a small handful of people, who have large vested interests in hundreds of unrelated conglomerates and people? Given the amount of money and influence at stake, common sense would suggest that any information that might damage the profits of their other companies, or influence of their stable of bought-and-paid-for people would be avoided or even ridiculed. And, as I write this book, we are just at the beginning of the "Fake News vs Real News" saga as well as outright censorship and maybe even taxation of the Internet.

I admit I am jaded when it comes to most media. I avoid the talking heads of the twenty-four-hour bad-news cycle, the establishment's agenda based "press-titutes" and their relentless fear mongering like the plague, because that's exactly what it is—a psychological plague. Just turn on your TV or go to your Internet homepage and you will find it riddled with negative misinformation and disinformation very carefully designed to protect and promote their people and corporations in an effort to sway public opinion in whatever way serves them. In fact, reporters that go against that agenda soon find themselves unemployed and unemployable. If being out of work isn't a strong enough reason to stick to their program, they find themselves threatened with embarrassment, bribery or even death. This isn't a conspiracy theory, it's a mafia tactic that's been going on for hundreds of years. Just do your research. Big money's stranglehold on the media is truly staggering, and the result on our collective consciousness is like a slow poison seeping silently into our water supply, day and night.

In fact, I'll go so far as to say that an addiction to being programmed regularly by the bad news media and their constant drone of negative news make your health, wealth and happiness extremely difficult, if not impossible, to attain. This is not mere speculation, but something I learned in workshops taught by the same psychologists that create and design much of our modern advertising. (FYI: a sick, financially enslaved and unhappy population creates billions of customers for some very profitable industries. Remember, to some, we are not seen as human beings but just potential income streams.)

Exercise: Avoid all forms of (mainstream and independent) news and media for one week and take note of how you feel and think without the contamination.

Bonus Exercise: Go on a smartphone detox for one week by pulling your battery and leaving your phone in your drawer at home. Check your messages only once per day for no more than 15 minutes. We are influenced by our "boxes" (smartphones, TVs, radios, et cetera) more than we realize.

Comfort Zones

How many psychologists does it take to change a light bulb?
Just one. But it has to want to change.

Funny joke, right? It's also very true.

Physics tells us that things want to keep doing what they are already doing. What direction are you moving in, or are you staying still? It largely depends on your habits. We are creatures of habit. Initially, every behavior or thought feels strange and uncomfortable, but with repetition we can become desensitized and get used to them. That's why both good and bad habits are hard to change.

Nearly everything we do, from our gestures and what we eat to the streets we regularly drive on and what we talk about, is influenced by our habits and comfort zones. Neurons that fire together wire together.

This is not a bad thing so long as these habits are producing the best results possible, and besides, if we had to think about every mundane thing we did all the time, we would become overloaded. So for the most part, we are in a type of low-grade trance, not really paying attention to most of what we do and why we are doing it, rarely asking what else or how else we could be doing things. But what if you are not getting the desired or best results? What if the market has changed since those techniques were developed? I caution you, you can become unconscious to both behaviors and results.

When we are confined to our comfort zones, we do not experience growth. In fact, any goal we set requires us to do some things we are not currently doing, otherwise it wouldn't be a goal! To reach a goal we must therefore form new habits, and to change habits, we must step outside our comfort zones.

At first, changing or ceasing to do the things we do on a regular basis can feel very awkward or even as if we are taking a step backward. However, if you look back on every goal you have ever achieved, you will see that it resulted from decisions you made and actions you took that were outside your comfort zones. The same will be true of any goals you achieve in the future.

Doing things over and over just because they are comfortable may not be always be a wise move. Growth requires that we become uncomfortable with both our results (what we are getting) and our activities (what we are doing). So be sure to reassess your results and activities on a regular basis, and learn to love feeling a little comfortably uncomfortable.

Exercise: For one week switch to your non-dominant hand for all activities, drive on different roads to work, go to a different religious ceremony, eat a food you're never eaten before, study a foreign language, watch YouTube videos about things you don't believe in and talk to people you normally ignore.

Common Sense Corner

In the corner:

- Treat others as you want to be treated.
- Eat less and move more.
- Under-promise and over-deliver.
- An ounce of prevention is worth a pound of cure.
- Measure twice cut once.
- Live within your means.
- If you sell to the need you don't need to sell.
- More sales actions leads to more sales income.
- If you want the skills do the drills.
- A penny saved is a penny earned.
- Think like an investor not a consumer.
- To be convincing you must be convinced.
- To be interesting, be interested.

These are simple yet overlooked credos for living successful, healthy and balanced lives. Unfortunately, common sense living isn't common!

Have you Been Immunized?— Jealousy and "Comparisonitis"

I was having lunch with my good friend Joe Girard and his wife Kitty when Joe suddenly grasped my hand, much in the way my father would, and in a concerned tone asked, "Duane, do you have the disease?"

Confused, I looked over to Kitty and asked, "What is Joe talking about?"

"Duane, the disease is a terrible thing," she replied cryptically, "It rarely spares anyone; in fact, we have lost most of our closest friends and family to it. Stay alert, because it can cause you a lot of suffering."

When they explained that the disease was jealousy, I sighed with relief.

"Don't worry about me," I told them, "I don't have a jealous bone in my body. I admire success. When someone is healthier, wealthier or happier than me, I want to know how did they did it so maybe I can get a little better myself."

Climbing the ladder to success is hard work, so hard in fact that you often don't notice that as you get closer to achieving success the pack has thinned out considerably. In fact, you will know you're doing well and making positive changes in your life when some of your friends and family members disappear and others even turn into haters. Maybe they are jealous, maybe they are afraid of losing you or maybe they are thinking you are judging them for not evolving in the same ways you are. Whatever their motivation, it can be a bit lonely when the people you're closest to become afflicted with jealousy.

As Joe and Kitty said, this disease is contagious and often fatal to your relationships. To avoid falling prey to it stop comparing yourself to others and instead start copying successful people's skills, habits and attitudes. Jealousy will not only cripple you, it will suck the enjoyment of life from you and everyone around you. There is no place in my life for it, for people that have it and hopefully not in yours either.

"Comparisonitis"

Another dangerous affliction—and an underlying cause of jealousy—is Comparisonitis. Its primary symptom is when one compares him or herself to others in any way and then finds that is followed by a rush of negative feelings. Sound familiar? If so, you are not alone. This ailment is rampant.

Even a mild version of comparisonitis can be debilitating and when combined with feelings of jealousy, it can be deadly. I've seen it kill families, partnerships, relationships and destroy the mental and physical health of those inflicted with it.

As soon as you start making changes, try to improve yourself or (heaven forbid) begin making real progress, many people around you (sometimes even your family and friends) will start falling victim to comparisonitis. Do *really well*, and some of them will morph into enemies. It's as though your success somehow threatens them. This is sad, but true. I know firsthand you won't know who your real friends and family are until you start to succeed. Misery may love company, but success can clear a room.

While comparisonitis is certainly a painful affliction it is also easily avoided. All you must do is make sure your only competition—in life and in business—is you. That way, you will always know exactly what your competition (you) is doing, what you are studying to become better, how hard you are working and what the price of your success really was.

So, when it comes to comparing, stick to comparing your younger self to the person you are today. And when you find someone who is better than you in any way, don't get jealous, get curious! Find out how they think and what they do so you can model their successful behavior.

I have sold many things to many very wealthy people and whenever the time and rapport feels right, I say something like "I totally admire how well you've done. Can I ask, what did your parents do?" If I find out their money is generational, knowing that just like lottery winners and professional athletes, only about one in ten people are able to keep or grow their inheritances, I then ask, "How did you keep or expand that money?" If they are self-made, my second question is, "How did you do it?" And I can tell you no one has ever told me about a banking or investment product of any kind (unless they were employed selling financial services!) What *did* they tell me? Well, that's exactly what I wrote about in detail in my book *Unstoppable Money*, and that's exactly how I handle my money now. Again, don't get jealous, get curious!

When I meet highly successful salespeople (and I've met thousands) I ask a similar question when the time is right: "How do you sell so well?" After observing them, modeling their suggestions and getting outstanding results, I then teach and train others on those strategies, all of which are documented in my book *The Six Sales Powers to Unstoppable Selling*.

Exercise: For one week, ask yourself, "How can I be a little better today than what I was yesterday, in any way?" And when you encounter someone who is better than you at something, say, "You are so amazing at that, it inspires me! How do you do it?"

Being Okay With Being the Tall Poppy

I started training and consulting when I worked for a Fortune 50 company. As part of a large team, I benefited from many "Train the Trainer" events and opportunities to discuss strategies and ideas with my colleagues. Before long, though, I had pulled ahead of them all to become arguably the most effective, engaging and prolific trainer within that company. I never knew why most of the others wanted to be trainers, but I was motivated by three primary things: the extensive and continuous travel meant an escape from the almost unbearable personal situation I was in at the time; I needed to get out from under two tyrant bosses (whom I despised) and prove they had incorrectly labeled me as incompetent; and I was committed to improving all my skills to such a high level that I would never again be reliant on anyone (except my customers) for my living. Needless, to say, I took what I learned—and what I taught—very, very seriously. I took on all the extra assignments, wrote all the courses, read all the books, modeled only the best people I could find and burned the midnight oil studying, all while on the road five to six days a week. When I look back at pictures from those years, I always had my lap top nearby. I was working almost every waking hour, and this positive distraction was very beneficial to me professionally and very healing to me personally.

At one of our Train the Trainer conferences, I was looking for my name tag but could not find it anywhere. Finally, after everyone was seated I found it at the back of the room, turned inside out and sarcastically renamed "Super Trainer." I looked around the room of about sixty other trainers and called out, "I don't know and I don't care who did this, but thank you! I proudly accept!"

As I mentioned earlier, an unfortunate early sign of success is resentment from your peers.

It's like the poppy farmers who walk their fields each morning with a pair of scissors to cut down the taller poppies that are growing too high above the others. When after years of blood, sweat and tears, you start to arrive at your goals, be prepared to deal with the tall poppy syndrome as friends and foe alike may try to cut you down.

Content vs. Intent

People won't remember what you said, but they are going to remember how you made them feel.

Remember, the meaning of your communication is seen in the results you are getting, so if you don't like the results, change your message and/or the way in which you deliver it. (FYI: when it comes to creating your own Unstoppable Attitude and how it affects you and others, you need to pay special attention to your internal communication.) For the most part, people are not listening to, nor will they remember, every word you say (your content). They will, however, relate and respond to your emotional message (your intent). Remember, your emotional message is the message or intent determines content.

Education and training focused solely on content is largely ineffective because it doesn't address how to use or deliver that information effectively, both internally and externally. Remember, the messenger affects the message. Your body language and tone affects everything you say and do in any type of communication, in any medium, because it affects the receiver's state. If you want to be a master communicator, you must become acutely aware of how your message is perceived and received. Then you'll be able to make changes to what you say (content) and how you say it (intent) until you start to get the result you want.

What you say and what you mean must be congruent, meaning your verbal and non-verbal communications must match up. Continually use your sensory acuity to calibrate your intent and content, just as you assess the way others communicate with you. To be convincing, you must be convinced.

Most importantly, remember that you cannot not communicate. You are always broadcasting to yourself internally and to the world externally through verbal and non-verbal cues, so pay attention to how you communicate with yourself!

Exercise: For one week become acutely aware of how your verbal and non-verbal communications are making those around you feel. Then for another week, select three very specific areas of interpersonal communications you want to improve and make a point of adjusting your approach until you start to get the reactions and results you want.

Gaining Credibility & Connection

If you are in sales, have you ever asked yourself why are the top salespeople the top sales people? For the most part, they have the highest credibility and the most connections in their communities. So if you want to become top in your field, you have to work on your credibility and connection every single day.

How can you improve your credibility? Tell the truth; know and live your trade; be dependable; under-promise and over-deliver; do not exaggerate; if you don't know something, admit it; and do not commit to a fact you're unsure of. In other words, say what you mean and mean what you say.

And how do you connect? People don't care how much you know until they know how much you care. You have to continually invest in the relationships you want and need in your life. Always observe the following tribal rules:

- People like and respect people like themselves.
- People like and respect people they want to be like.
- People like and respect people that seem to like them.
- People do business with people they like and respect.
- People like and respect people who dislike and disrespect the same people.

It's much easier to maintain your Unstoppable Attitude if you create and sustain your credibility and connection with those you interact with and rely on most often.

The Five-Second, Five-Question Daily Development Program

My experience has shown me that our personality, quality of being and life results can be developed through daily reflection, analysis and cultivation. Oftentimes it's as simple as asking ourselves a few questions. Quality questions create a quality life.

Below are the five questions I ask myself each and every day, and I promise that over time, you will notice some amazing results if you do the same.

1. How do I want my day to be?

2. What do I have to do today?

3. How am I doing with all my interactions?

4. How do I want my evening to be?

5. What two things did I do well yesterday, and what two things could I have done better?

After years of asking myself these questions and teaching them to countless others, I can honestly say that no one has ever said they wanted their day to be "lousy," "boring" or "unproductive." However, I do commonly hear things like "great!", "fun!", "chill!", "awesome!", "powerful!", "relaxed!", "focused!", "centered!", "brilliant!", "productive!" and "money!" Why? Because our nature is to learn, love, have fun and experience joy! There is no better time than today, so stop majoring in minor things and start moving towards the person you were meant to be!

Exercise: Close your eyes, take a deep breath, and ask yourself those five questions every single morning before you leave your home. Take note of any changes that occur in how you think, act, react or feel. Why should you do this daily? Because it's free, fast, easy, and it works. The world around us is conditioning us to accept less, so we need to condition ourselves even harder to become more. With laser beam focus, you have to be crazier than the world around you or the world around you will eat you up!

The Downside of Don't

In the English language, the word "don't" is a negator, which means that when you use that word it forces you to focus on, or visualize, whatever it is you're trying to avoid.

"Don't picture chocolate almonds in a gold dish." What did you just see?

This is a subtle but powerful thing to understand when it comes to motivational psychology. If you are trying to quit smoking and all you say to yourself is "I don't want to smoke" you're going to picture yourself smoking, which in all likelihood will actually increase your cravings.

If you want to achieve a goal, you have to focus on what you want and the new behaviors you will have to take on. Instead of saying to yourself, "I don't want to smoke" you might try saying, "My lungs are free, clear and pink" or "I breathe deep clean air anytime I think about smoking". This works for anything, even managing people. For example, instead of saying to your children, "Don't spill the milk," (which will cause them to visualize and reinforce a milk spilling pattern) say, "Carry the milk carefully."

I will never forget the time I was working in British Columbia, and brought my nephew along on a small golf vacation. While we were having lunch, I noticed a server rounding the corner, a large tray of empty dishes in her hand. The manager barked, "Don't drop the dishes!" And, right on cue, as if she were given a direct command, the entire tray fell from her hands.

Exercise: Do a social experiment. For one week, try new language patterns on the people around you, for example, "Don't laugh at my jokes" or "Don't think about how much we have in common" or "Don't think about all my awesome qualities." Then watch their reaction. Have fun with this one, but use your powers for good, not evil, my Jedi!

"When you look at the dark side, careful you must be. For the dark side looks back."

—*Yoda*

E-Motion

The etymology of the word emotion relates to how feeling and movement are connected. For most of us, most of the time, how we move affects how we feel. In other words, many of us feel what we feel because we move in ways that access those states. If I asked you to describe how a depressed person breathes, stands, sits, tilts their heads, uses their hands and moves their feet, I'm fairly certain we would all describe the same motions. However, what many people don't realize is that some people are not moving that way because they are depressed, they are depressed because they habitually move that way! So just by changing your habitual body language you can change your habitual emotions! Like everything else I write about, I know this from firsthand experience. Change how you move and you will change how you feel.

When I was a teenager, I was referred to by one of my coaches as a "sidewalk counter." I would walk looking down as if I were counting the cracks in the sidewalk, and I had a permanent brooding scowl on my face. When I read that our body language affects our habitual state of mind, it instantly rang true for me. With my athletic background, I already knew that in martial arts and yoga the primary mode of quickly changing your state of mind is adjusting your physiology, but I had never thought to expand that wisdom to outside the dojo or studio and into my daily life.

I decided to conduct an experiment. I asked myself, how do

people who are usually in a great mood sit, walk, stand and move? Then I held these images in my mind and emulated them, paying special attention to my posture, pace, facial expressions, muscle tension and stance. Almost instantly, and somewhat miraculously, I noticed my state of mind shifting along with my body. In fact, understanding and honoring these simple and effective laws led to some of my very first major shifts in attitude, and ability to manage my attitude at will, until this day.

Even more fascinating is the fact that people mirror you. That means your body language can influence their state, the flow of conversation, and their feelings associated with you. This is how you subtly build or lose rapport, so be aware of it. When people are comfortable with each other, their movements will entrain, or match each other, for good or for bad.

One of the simplest ways to gain rapport is to match and mirror the body language of the other person. Once you have done this, you can then lead them into whatever state you wish, simply by changing your physiology or motion. When you change your motion, you affect your emotion and that of others around you.

Note also that our bodies are made up mostly of O_2 and H_2O, and when these primary fuels are in short supply our attitude machine is one of the first things affected. So don't forget to stay hydrated and take some deep breaths all day long.

Exercise: Sit up in your chair, look straight up at the ceiling, repeatedly smile, nod, say yes, breathe and try to create negative thoughts or feelings while looping this physiology over and over (good luck!). Then, sit leaning on your knees with your elbows, completely drop your head, mostly close your eyes, move your head slowly from side to side, mumble no and try to feel cheery (almost impossible!). Trying to cross your neurological wires like this really proves how connected our thoughts and feelings are to our body language.

Levitation through Meditation

In my opinion, YouTube is quite possibly the most wonderful technology for entertainment and education to come along in my lifetime, so let's hope censorship, user fees, taxation and regulation stay away! I have probably learned more real world information and skills listening to YouTube while driving my car (attending "Autoversity," as I call it and now post videos to YouTube under that name) in the last two years, than I did attending formal school for ten. Many videos help with my skills and are also great for maintaining my Unstoppable Attitude. For example, Jerry Seinfeld "cracks me up" and the young Arnold Schwarzenegger videos "pump me up." Oddly enough, these two very different characters came together one day to introduce me to one of my favorite daily activities.

While listening to YouTube I came across separate interviews, years apart, in which Jerry and Arnold were discussing the many benefits of Transcendental Meditation (TM), crediting it for much of their focus, ability to handle stress and vitality. Intrigued, I conducted a little research and learned that the training entailed just three group classes and a private session with the instructor. I signed up for the training and since then have practiced TM for twenty minutes once or twice a day, with profound benefits.

When I practice it daily my stress levels are almost non-existent, my body feels better and I am much more relaxed, capable, focused, patient, productive and centered. Quite a return on twenty minutes—just ask me, Jerry, Arnold and about a billion other people around the world, this really works!

Exercise: Find a quiet spot, put in some earplugs and sit comfortably in a chair, or car (not while you're driving, of course), and close your eyes. Then, simply repeat a monotone word over and over and over in your mind, without moving any part of your mouth. It does not matter what the word is, so long as it is neutral, meaning it does not have any significance for you, negative or positive. This meaningless word is called your mantra. If your thoughts begin to drift or if you feel drowsy just bring your mind back to the repetition of that word. You don't need to focus on your breathing or anything else. The repetition of that neutral word occupies your analytical mind while your spacial mind lets go and drifts off, the result of which is a deep relaxed state that is nothing short of incredible. I do recommend taking a class and learning this from a master TM teacher, who will also assign you your unique repetitive mantra or word.

"If every eight-year-old in the world is taught meditation, we will eliminate violence from the world within one generation."

—*The Dalai Lama*

Seek Music, Humor, Nature and Avoid Energy Takers

The benefits of putting ourselves in a positive environment for a few minutes a day cannot be underestimated. It is also well-documented—a quick Google, Bing or Yahoo search will turn up a plethora of articles, books and studies on how laughing, walking in nature or listening to uplifting music can change your entire outlook and even inspire you to dream up and achieve your goals. So get outside as often as you can, put on whatever tunes speak to your heart, and be sure to laugh at something every single day. In simple terms, revert to how you were as a child. On the flip side, steer clear as much as possible from people who drain your energy and bring you down.

Exercise: Find some of your favorite music or clips of a side-splitting comedy routine, load it onto your phone, then play it each day while you are walking outside and away from anyone who brings you down!

Three Barriers

There are three main barriers to success: fear, habits and laziness. Fear of success, failure, embarrassment or trying something new. Habits that are so ingrained that change seems impossible. Laziness or lack of motivation and the physical energy to take action.

Exercise: Review your goals and assess how you are doing with them. Determine which one of these three things is preventing you from really working towards each goal and then write the letters F, H or L (sometimes you'll find it's all three) beside them. This is a great diagnostic exercise to find out what is holding you back.

Remember, self-awareness is the first step toward change.

IQ, EQ and OQ

I started to research these terms a few years ago and was fascinated with what I learned.

Intelligence Quotient is essentially a measurement of how quickly and how well you can identify patterns. Go online and take two or three free IQ tests, then research how IQ scores correlate to one's success in life and business. What you find may surprise you. Generally, people with *extremely low* and *extremely high* IQs do equally poorly in life. Those with very low IQs tend to lack the horsepower for complex activities, while extremely high IQ people often spend so much time analyzing, scrutinizing and criticizing every plan that they seldom take action. It is also a relatively static thing throughout our lives and somewhat out of our control, so maybe you have been blessed with an average IQ. After all, when you're lost you want to be smart enough to read the map, but not so smart as to doubt everything on it!

Emotional Quotient is a measurement of your resiliency, how well you handle adversity, and how grateful you are for even the smallest of opportunities. Think of it as a compass; it is a good indication of where you are headed and the quality of your experiences while you are on the journey. Highly successful people, families, companies and even countries tend to have high EQs. The great news is that unlike your IQ you can control your EQ by changing how you react to and interpret things. Over the years, I have cultivated and developed my sense of gratitude, resiliency and ability to handle adversity, and I continue to work on it.

Openness Quotient is a measurement of how open-minded you are, which thankfully is in your control as well. Since the mark of an intelligent mind is the ability to entertain any thought without judging it, you can see how important it is to continually push your OQ. As Tom Campbell rightly asserts, the key is to always be both open-minded (so you will look at and consider anything that may help you empower yourself or others), but skeptical (so you don't just buy into everything you are exposed to).

So let's all raise our glasses to average IQs, high OQs and massive EQs. Cheers!

Evolve or Dissolve

The only constant is change. Change is a certainty, but progress is not.

Exercise: Have some fun with this one! Close your eyes and go through, in slow deep detail and with emotion, what it would be like to live a full day in the shoes of the following people:

- **A nomad in Mongolia, 10,000 years ago.**

- **A young, gun-slinging law keeper of a frontier town in the American Old West, 1745.**

- **A poor young woman trapped in a bad marriage to a much older, wealthy man, in France, 1810.**

- **A young man collecting intel on possible government threats in Chicago, 1943.**

What you will find is everyone in every era had very different challenges and opportunities and that they had to adapt to the constant changes in their environments throughout their lives. This exercise creates empathy for other people from different eras and unfamiliar environments. It will help open your mind and realize challenging human conditions are shared by everyone across all ages and environments.

If you, your relationships and your business don't evolve, they will dissolve before their time. So what's easier, the pain of discipline (evolving) or the pain of regret (dissolving)? Making changes is never easy but it is far less costly than becoming irrelevant, stale or redundant.

For the record, I'm not too sure about "evolution" in general. I don't see any evidence of living systems getting better and better, or us getting smarter and smarter. As a matter of fact, in the general geological, archeological written and genetic records, you could argue that society, people and many other things in nature devolve now and then. But I do think there is plenty of evidence of *adaptation*. Those people and creatures that adapt the quickest and best to the varied situations presented to them have the greatest chance to survive and thrive.

How are you adapting to your current environment, business climate and changes in your life?

Focus and Flow

Exercise: Take one minute to really observe your surroundings. Notice everything that is black, then close your eyes and verbally list as many things of these black items as you can. Next, without opening your eyes, try to list everything that is blue. Notice the difference in your ability to recall what is blue. Now open your eyes and take one minute to find everything that is blue. I would be willing to bet you over looked much of the blue items.

This is a simple but effective exercise to illustrate how our energy flows where our focus goes. In order for you to find the color black, you have to look right past all the other colors.

What does this have to do with your attitude? You will always find more of what you focus on because focusing on one thing always comes at the expense of looking past other things. If you focus on the *can'ts, won'ts, shouldn'ts, wouldn'ts and couldn'ts*, that's all you'll see—obstacles. On the other hand, if you focus on the *cans, wills, shoulds, woulds, and coulds* you will find you will notice—and be presented with—more opportunities.

It is for this reason that we must always focus on what we can do, not what we can't do. If you focus on the negatives of your job, body, skills, habits, partner, products, prices, economy or whatever, you will be distorting reality, making those things overly large focal points and disempowering yourself because you have to look past all the positives.

Focus is a matter of choice and habit. Problem-solvers are realists and being a realist requires you to see things as they are, no better, and certainly no worse.

Flies and Bees

Honeybees are attracted to flowers and make honey.

Flies are attracted to shit and make maggots.

I have never seen a honeybee attracted to shit or a fly attracted to a flower. It's a natural law.

(Reader, I could have used the word feces or poop above, but those words lack the energy necessary to convey the message. Sometimes, you have to just say it like it is, even when it may seem inappropriate.)

Since people tend to like people similar to themselves, pay close attention to the type of people you're attracting and why.

We all want to be liked by others. But know this: an indication that you are winning the game of life is when negative people are repelled by you. You have flowers to grow and honey to make, so let those flies land on a pile of manure somewhere else and start making maggots far from you!

We practice this at my company. The people working with me often say that we have the best customers who are kind and grateful! We have "honeybee" clients. Flies seldom buzz around us, and when they do we have no problem shooing them away.

Look at the people around you and then look in the mirror. This natural law of attraction explains who is drawn to you, repulsed by you, and why.

I'm OK with being respected but not liked by everyone.

Energy Givers = Honey Bees. Energy Takers = Flies.

FLIP Out!

"FLIP" is an easy acronym to remember if you want to check and change your state, as well as the state of others.

"F" stands for focus. What are you focusing on? Seeking pleasure or avoiding pain, winning more or losing less, doing things to increase your odds for success or reduce your chance of failure? Focus on what you can learn in any situation. Focus on your goals, gratitudes, body language, dominant thoughts or anything else you can control. Start noticing what you focus on and work on directing that focus throughout your day.

"L" stands for language. This pertains to how we talk to others and ourselves. Examples of poor self-talk include, "Why am I surrounded by idiots?" or "Why do I get all the bad customers?" Positive self-talk would be things like "I will make some contacts so I can book an appointment!" or "What can I study to improve my skill set?" You will search for answers and evidence for any question you ask yourself or statement you make to yourself. This of course affects your focus and your state, so choose your internal language wisely. Speak to others with care. You could say things like, "You irritate me," and "Will you get out of my face?" or "I find your approach interesting," and "Let's go over this another time okay?" The way you speak to others can drastically affect your business and personal relations so choose your questions and statements wisely.

"I" pertains to intensity. How much energy and intensity

do you bring to your day and dealings with others? Your intensity needs to be situationally appropriate but make sure you have enough vitality and intensity for long enough periods to really impact and benefit yourself and others.

Finally, the "P" is your physiology. Your physiology drives your Focus, Language and Intensity so pay very close attention to it. Your posture, facial expressions and pace of movement are fundamental mood drivers as they directly and instantly affect your brain chemistry and neurology. And because people mirror each other, your attitude is contagious to others; they will subconsciously match your body language, positive or negative. In addition pay close attention to your patterns of hydration, breathing and nutrition. We are mostly water and oxygen so if you're feeling tired or flat, drink some water and go for a brisk walk, allowing your arms to swing, your gait to be fluid, look straight ahead or up and smile, and be sure to take some deep breaths. I would also research what has been discovered about the potential benefits of taking certain supplements and the power balanced gut bacteria flora has on your ability to ward off the blues and keep your attitude machine functioning at its best!

Exercise: Write the acronym FLIP on a piece of paper and place it on your bathroom mirror. By noticing and adjusting your FLIP you can influence your mood and state in real time as effectively as a master musician plays an instrument. Unfortunately we weren't born with an owner's manual that shows us how to run this magnificent machine of ours for maximum performance but be grateful you have finally found some practical tools that you can use to benefit yourself and others every single day!

Four Elements of Prosperity

Every successful person who has experienced significant successes has managed four things. What are they?

The first element is vision. This is different from mere left brain goal-setting. A vision is a very real internal holographic image or blueprint of what you want to move toward. It is compelling and embedded with all your motivating *whys*. When you think of your vision, you feel it in your body. When this vision becomes clear to you, you will not just want it, you will crave it!

The second element is your state or mood. For example, if you are trying to persuade someone, you must be able to increase your target's acceptance levels and buying energy until they are ready to say yes, and since you cannot give something that you do not have, you have to maintain a high level of energy. Remember, you and only you hold the keys to your attitude machine, so use the tools in this book to keep your engines running and your tank full of gas.

The third element is belief. As mentioned earlier, we all have belief systems that drive what we think we can or cannot do. These beliefs develop into a personal story we keep telling ourselves about who we are, what we are capable of, why we do things and how our lives will play out. And, if not empowering, these limiting beliefs will form a jail cell, imprisoning us with its invisible bars. If your belief system or personal story does not match the direction you want your life to take, you may need to recreate it.

The fourth element is strategy. Strategy pertains to mechanics. Since mechanics and strategy is only one of four elements, please note that three-fourths of your success is psychology: your vision, state and beliefs! We tend to focus a lot on strategies but the reality is that you can't execute even the best strategies without a consistent and compelling vision, a strong state and effective beliefs!

Exercise: Hold a personal or professional goal in mind. Grab a pen and paper and take your time to DEEPLY assess that goal in all four areas mentioned above: Vision, State, Belief and Strategy.

Four Levels of Development

Many years ago I purchased my first jet ski. I remember being so excited as my young family piled into the car and we headed down toward the marina. Joy soon turned to frustration when I attempted to reverse my trailer down the marina launch pad. I couldn't get it into the water to save my life. The ramps were crowded that day and after several minutes of being ogled by onlookers and impatient boaters I had to admit defeat. Embarrassed and frustrated, I left and drove to a nearby mall parking lot to practice my trailering reverse skills. I was what you would call an "Unconscious Incompetent," meaning I went to the marina that day completely unaware of how much I didn't know. I continued my exposure and progressed to the second level....

Over the next several visits to the lake, I transitioned into a "Conscious Incompetent," meaning I was becoming aware of all the things I didn't know and was therefore in a position to improve upon them. Is there any area in your life that you are just now beginning to realize all the things you don't know about? If so, you probably know you need and want training and practice, just like I did. Then I moved to the third level…

Within a short period of time and practice, I moved into becoming a "Conscious Competent," meaning I could use the trailer well but still had to think about everything I was doing while backing it down the ramp. Are there things that you do well but still must concentrate on in order to complete? Depending on the frequency and intensity of the activity, you may stay in this stage forever. Over the years, I have slid into the fourth level...

With repetition and focus you can eventually reach the fourth level of development: "Unconscious Competent." This means you are so proficient at the task that you don't have to think about it. You may even be able to multitask while doing it without sacrificing the quality. What complex activities can you do without even thinking about? While this is indeed a wonderful feeling, there is the risk of becoming bored or complacent. When you find yourself operating at this level, find a way to teach that skill to others. This will keep things new and exciting for you; it will also require you to analyze your practices and stay conscious of your habits.

Funny Fruits and Vegetables

Is there someone you would rather not have to deal with at work, family functions or even pass by in the hall? We all have people who rub us the wrong way, and much as we'd like to, we are not always able to eliminate them from our lives. But did you know that by changing the way you internally represent this person and associate different things with them, you could also change your feelings toward them and it can even be fun!

Advertisers and political spin doctors spend a lot of time and money researching and deploying how to change the way we associate things. For instance, there were ads a few decades ago that would show "credentialed" doctors promoting smoking and "loving" mothers giving their babies soda pop in baby bottles! This may seem ridiculous to us now, but I can assure you people will look back at some of our consumer behavior today and find them completely ridiculous as well! The point here is, if you change what you associate things to, you immediately change how you feel and respond to them and this affects what actions you will or won't take.

Exercise: Think of a fruit or vegetable you find silly or funny. Any piece of produce that makes you giggle a little will do. Now close your eyes and picture a person that irritates you. Imagine cropping off their head and pushing their body to the side. Now take that silly produce

and slide it under the image of their head, so the produce is now their body. Take a deep breath and lock this image into your mind. This is now how you will permanently represent this person in your mind. How does that feel? I bet it feels a lot better!

Any time you think about this person, look at them or need to be around them, reference this new image. You will notice an immediate change in how you feel about them and how you react to them. And they will notice the difference and react differently to you as well. Change the associations you have about anything and you change your feelings, instantly.

Perhaps more importantly, this exercise illustrates the point I made earlier about fighting with our thoughts. When you try not to think about the person you don't like, all you do is think about them more, and likely with growing irritation. However, when you replace your original thoughts and patterns with a new one, you change your perception and reactions accordingly.

Are you asking yourself why simple effective and free patterns like these aren't taught in school? Keep asking yourself, but remember to follow the money…there is no big money to be made from these self-help remedies and once successful, they eliminate the need for many products and services in several multi-billion dollar industries. Just a thought.…

Win the GAFF and Gas Awards

Warning: this tip is rated R for profanity.

Have you ever walked out of a business and said to yourself, "Wow, they really don't seem to give a F@#*!? I'm certainly not going to give them my money!" I know I have, whenever I get the feeling that I am not valued as a customer.

As a business owner or salesperson, your goal is to have the highest GAFF in your market. GAFF stands for the "Give A F@#* Factor," and if you have it you're probably well on your way to owning your market, if you don't already.

How do you know if you have huge GAFF? You display it! You do the little things like opening the door for your clients; remembering what they take in their coffee; wishing your customers a happy birthday; putting a little skip in your step when you walk away to get them something; taking extra care to pronounce and spell their name properly; smiling and nodding when talking and listening; making notes of important information; bringing the product to them instead of making them go to the product; and having tons of customer service energy and natural enthusiasm. I could go on and on.

If you work for a company and consistently display GAFF, you will likely be considered the employee with the most GAS. This distinction is reserved for those who Give A SH#@ day in and day out, going above and beyond for the customer and the company. When you have GAFF and GAS, nothing can stop you!

I should warn you, having GAFF and GAS will bring about drastic changes in your career and your life, including:

- Being promoted and getting raise after raise.
- Getting headhunted for more money.
- Repeat and referral business starts pouring in.

If you compete against yourself every day, increasing your GAS and GAFF, you will make it very hard for your competition to compete against you!

Head, Heart, Gut

While many believe that decision-making is just an intellectual process, it is actually far more than that.

Have you ever seen someone hold their heart and say, "I just love it!" or put their arms on their gut and say, "Give me some time to get a feel for this" or hold their head and say, "I' m trying to process this." They are unconsciously expressing what science has proved: our bodies are loaded with brain neurons (have you ever heard of muscle memory?) with the highest concentration of neurons in our head, heart and gut. (In fact, there is mounting scientific evidence that neurons may only be the receivers and transmitters of information, *not* the *creators* of it. It's like we have been given three separate computers to help us navigate our lives that are able to download and upload information to some unseen source.) When we understand the computational power of using our head, heart AND gut to make decisions, we see situations with more clarity and are much more able to make better decisions.

Exercise: Think of a decision you are struggling with, or ask someone you know who is struggling with a decision to do this exercise with you. Hold the problem in mind, then put your hand on your head and ask it, "Should I do this, yes or no?" After you get your yes or no, using a scale of 1 to 10, where 1 is weak and 10 is strong, ask, "How strong is that yes or no?" Then move on to your heart and your gut, repeating those steps with each of them.

This is one of the most profound tools I have ever created, and it never ceases to amaze me in its wisdom and accuracy. Reasonable minds can debate about *how* it works, but the fact that it does is, in my experience, not up for argument. I've used it to guide many personal and professional decisions for myself and countless others, and it has always worked perfectly.

Some warnings:

- Don't allow your head, heart and gut to "talk" to each other or try to sell each other on their own type of justifications (It's actually very odd to sense when this is happening).

- Majority rules, meaning when two out of three are in agreement the decision has been made. That said, you want to take into account the strength of the decision on the 1 to 10 scale.

- Never, ever make a decision out of fear, ego, when experiencing hormonal shifts or while intoxicated, as those factors distort or shut down your three decision centers.

Here is synchronicity at it's best: I am sitting in a Starbucks around the corner from my client doing my final review of this book before it goes to print with my publisher. As I sat down I accidentally dialed someone that has been causing some conflicts in my life, I have been torn about how to handle them. I open my word document, and the first chapter I have to review is this one. So I just did a head, heart and gut review asking the question "should I continue to try to work with this person?" and my head, heart and gut all came in as an instant and solid NO. Wow, my ego and fear were getting the best of me, what a relief to be done with that decision.

We are all born with three computers, so why not train ourselves to use all three effectively and efficiently?

Incantations

An incantation is anything you repeat, over and over, in your head or out loud. You know, those thoughts that run in a loop through your mind. Over time, incantations have the power to define you, your attitude, and how you see and react to your world.

Optimists use inCANtations and pessimists use inCAN-Tations. Whatever you impress on your mind regularly, will automatically show up in your life and business, so be sure to pay close attention to your internal and external looping language and design this powerful strategy to your advantage.

This is not about wishful thinking or trying to bring about an impossibility by stating it over and over again (for example, stating over and over again that you are very tall is not going to change the fact that you may be below-average height).

An incantation is you convincing yourself that you are developing the traits, are doing the activities or are getting the results you want. It is essential that you create and reinforce with emotion inCANtations such as, "I'm a great salesperson", "I put only nutritious foods into my body", "I am lean and muscular" or "Every day in any several ways I am getting better and better." When you focus on these thoughts, you will find negative inCANTations such as "I'm not good enough," "They won't like me," or "This offer won't be accepted" will decrease in frequency, intensity and eventually disappear altogether.

Since the easiest way to create change is to replace a behavior by starting something new rather than trying to just stop something, designing and using customized incantations will allow you to program your thoughts and behaviors just as easily as installing new software on a computer.

Exercise: Look at your goals. Choose who or what you want or need to become and visualize it. Set an hourly timer on your phone, and everytime it goes off, say the phrase, "I am that I am!" to yourself with conviction, emotion and congruity while holding that image of your better future self in mind. Do this for one month.

Decide to Decide!

When we are going through difficult times, we often feel powerless. But the reality is most of the time, our struggles are not the result of us being powerless, it's because we won't exercise our power and simply make a decision.

Incision means to cut into. Decision means to cut off. When a judge makes a decision, they have cut off your future from any other possibilities. Maybe that's why it can seem so scary! That said, once you start to make more decisions with the right intention, you will find making even more decisions becomes easier as you begin to reap the rewards and develop your "decision making muscles." Small decisions will naturally lead to ever bigger decisions, so don't delay and start making even tiny decisions today!

Exercise: Think of an unproductive habit you engage in. Picture it as a weed, intruding on your garden and choking off the flowers of your inspiring ideas, then make a decision to uproot or cut the weed off *today*. Then, after taking some time to acknowledge the positive change in your life (there will always be at least one) and realize how easy it is to effect change, decide to cut off another unproductive habit and pull that weed as well. Then just keep looking for more weeds in your life and keep cutting them down and pulling them out, and just like in a garden, this will create lots of room for more flowers to grow.

"Tiny positive or negative increments in the quality of your intent and decisions, over many thousands of choices, eventually lead to either an increasing or decreasing quality of consciousness."

—Tom Campbell

Goals vs. Intentions

An intention is like an impotent goal, for it lacks the assertion a real goal has. Take New Year's resolutions for example. If you're like most people, you've probably noticed that many of these resolutions tend to fall by the wayside within a few days or weeks after the holiday season. Why? Because they are more like New Year's *intentions*.

Imagine you are on a boat. The boat has suddenly lost its power and you've begun to drift off to sea. The land is getting further and further in the distance. If you have just an intention to get back, you might try to paddle and maybe even swim a little. An intention is a low-grade desire. Now, if you had a burning goal to get back this is very different. Goals are structured as personal musts and are typically reinforced by large personal *whys*, or reasons to reach the goal. If getting back was really a goal, you would try anything!

Never confuse intentions with goals; it dilutes your power. To help you clarify, write down your goals, along with your motivating whys. Struggling to come up with the whys is perhaps a good indication that this is just an intention and should be taken off your goal list, as a goal will easily inspire your many reasons and whys to achieve it. If you have enough "Whys" the "Hows" become easy!

Heroes

Here are three outstanding ways to get some clear direction and gain some much-needed leverage over yourself:

Get some heroes.

Ask yourself, "Who do I want to be like? Who do I know, or who can I find that has already achieved what I want to achieve? What traits do they possess that helped bring them their successes?" This does not mean that you need to become this person; in fact, you don't even have to like them! You do however want to emulate their specific traits that relate to the attainment of your goals. In moments of doubt remind yourself that your hero / role model struggled at some points with his or her goal as well! But if they can do it why can't you? You may even find that you can do it faster than they did because you have their proven blueprint to follow and know what to do with precision as you are avoiding their years of painful learning using trials, errors and experiences.

Get some anti-heroes.

Ask any successful person about their journey and they will tell you they learned from their mistakes. But did you know you can also learn from their mistakes? Ask yourself, "Who do I not want to be like? Who has failed in the areas in which I wish to succeed? Who has made some significant mistakes in their life that I would like to avoid?" These people are our anti-heroes, and they show us what not to do, how not to think and how not to act. In other words, what to precisely move away from. This is not a time to judge. You are simply trying to identify who has not gotten the results you want or who has gotten lost along the way, and why. Then you can make a mental note of what not to do, of what you want to move away from. You will find that whenever you start acting like that person, an alarm bell will go off in your mind, warning you to stop and change direction.

As you make your lists of heroes and anti-heroes, you may find that certain individuals occupy a spot on both, albeit for different reasons. This has happened to me several times as I studied people's activities, beliefs, behaviors, traits and results. For example, I had a sales and sales training hero who was also my ethics and morality anti-hero. He was both highly skilled and highly unethical, and I was able to pick and choose what I wanted to model and what I wanted to avoid, as I got to see firsthand how things turned out for him for both good and bad.

Be a hero.

Think back to the section on "Take Your Child to Work Day." It was about thinking and behaving in a way that you would want your child to witness and emulate. But you don't have to be a parent to be a role model. Imagine how great it would be to have someone—be it a friend, colleague or relative—look back at their lives or careers and say, "Wow, I am very grateful you were in my life at that time!" By viewing yourself as a role model, you help others while raising your own bar.

Remember, attitude and success is nothing but a big mind game that you are playing with yourself all the time; the question is, are you playing to win or lose? This book is really about mastering more inner games so you can start to win more outer games!

Exercise: Grab a pen, paper and your Gratitude and Goal list. On the paper, write down the words Hero, Anti-hero and Be A Hero, and start working on your hero lists. Think about people you know and others you have heard about, as they relate to your Goal list and see who fits where. Don't rush yourself, and don't be surprised as names continue to come to you throughout the week.

I will never forget the day my mother said "Duane, I don't know how you did it, but you seem to have taken the best traits from both your father and I, and somehow have not picked up either of our bad habits." I smiled, nodded and told her it was because of this practice. Choose who and how you want to be and start designing yourself and your life right now!

Hetero and Auto Suggestion

Our expectations, beliefs, values and identity have been directly and indirectly imprinted on us by things such as the language and body language of our family, friends, teachers, customers, co-workers, teammates, society, country, region, city, media, social media, music, advertising, books, magazines, movies, stories, nursery rhymes, songs, poetry, religion and ethnic groups, to name just a few. This imprinting is known as hetero-suggestion, and it encompasses all of the programming and training we are exposed to throughout our lives. Studies have shown that it begins before birth, through the chemical, emotional, kinesthetic, visual and auditory environment of our mother's womb. (That said, there are also billions of people around the world who believe that we carry experiences, thoughts and consequences from our past lives.)

The point is, you are being programmed, or trained, all the time and in a multitude of ways. It could be as subtle as an unsupportive facial expression you received the last time you told someone one of your goals or how you interpreted your doctor's tone of voice when they gave you "the news."

Simply becoming aware that hetero-suggestion is happening will give you an entirely new perspective on your life. You may even start to notice when it is happening and be able to decide whether you want to be imprinted and how to react to this imprinting. Without this basic awareness however, you are like a blank canvas walking around a studio of painters with wet brushes. We are often in a vulnerable hypnagogic state, which is a very open, relaxed and highly suggestive state of mind.

Most people go through their lives unaware that they are being programmed by such mundane things as television shows, commercials, websites and the music they expose themselves to. It has also been shown that the more you use your smartphone, or even spend around smartphones (and therefore exposing yourself to their brain entrained frequencies), the more time you are spending in a trance-like nether world and are even more susceptible to hetero-suggestive brainwashing.

Now that you are aware of hetero-suggestion, you can counter it with auto-suggestion. Auto-suggestion is what you tell yourself about yourself, including who and what you are and will become. Whatever you repeatedly tell yourself, especially with conviction and emotion, you will move toward. Be it positive or negative, moving forwards or backwards, you do become what you think about.

Hetero and Auto suggestion, FLIP, the placebo/nocebo effect, beliefs, goals, gratitudes, incantations, blueprints, ANTs, affirmations and so many other concepts in this book come together in a holistic and comprehensive way, like a web with you and your better future at its center. Remember real success is ¾ psychology and only ¼ mechanics.

Exercise: For one day, stay vigilantly alert to all the direct and indirect programming you are either accidentally or purposely exposed to, overtly or covertly. It will shock you. Then, if you like, try to determine the intention behind some of it. Those of you who are particularly naïve (as I was), may find yourself shocked as you realize the extent of this in our lives and our world. Again, consider following the money...since knowledge is potential power, I hope you use these new insights to help empower you and others, and start to become acutely aware of all the societal programming and all the hetero-suggestive techniques that surround us.

Hocus Focus—Two Almost Magical Relaxations

Your mind can flutter around so incredibly fast you may be fooled into believing you can hold several simultaneous thoughts at one time. The reality is, you can focus your mind on only one thing at a time, however brief each thought may be. Moving between several ideas just milliseconds apart from each other will lead most of us to mental fatigue, declaring, "We have a lot on our minds!" We can give our mind a rest by putting it to work on a single task.

Here are two of my favorite exercises to train your brain, reduce distress and improve what's known as mindfullness (self awareness of your own mind ... which could lead one to the natural question, "So what is it that observes your mind?)

Exercise 1—Walking: While walking, focus keenly on how your breath, heart and entire upper body feel. Then move your attention to how your leg bones feel. Then to all your muscles and tendons. Followed by how your entire foot feels while it strikes the earth. Then your foot in your shoe. And finally the sounds of your foot as it strikes the ground and within your body. Firmly move your mind to those areas in sequence. Repeat.

Exercise 2—Breathing. Sit quietly, close your eyes and focus completely on the feeling and sound of your own breath during every inhale and exhale. Breathe in a color that represents abundance, and exhale a color that represents cleansing; whatever colors you choose are the right colors for you. Repeat.

How far and long can you go without any other thoughts entering your mind? These exercises are much more difficult than they seem, so don't be discouraged. When done repetitively over time, your skills will impove while the many mental and physical health benefits will become self-evident. These strategies are thousands of years old and if ineffective I assume would have been lost and forgotten eons ago.

The practices of Yoga and Tai Chi use precise, slow and complex movements which require you to fixate your thoughts on a single point as you move through the sequences. Often referred to as "moving meditations," the benefits they bring to your mind, body and attitude should not be overlooked.

Contrary to popular myth, meditation is rarely about clearing your mind but more about giving your mind an assignment and focusing on that task with increasing frequency and intensity.

Image-In

Did you know that images conjured in our minds create reactions in our nervous systems as if they were actually happening? I have seen two-hundred-fifty-pound men freeze when handed the phone and told to take or make calls with me, even after hours of training. What is a fear of the phone? Are they literally afraid of the phone? Were they physically attacked by a phone at some point? No, their true fear is whatever they have "imaged-in" or imagined happening on the phone and it was affecting them physically.

What do you tend to image-in? Is it eating a certain food, getting along better with your spouse, arguing with neighbors, buying a car or paying off the credit card? Creating a personal image board, with pictographs and pictures of how you want your life to be is a very literal imaging-in of what you want to become. This method can be very successful, particularly for visual learners because you are actually inserting yourself into the story you have created every time you look at the board.

Exercise: Get a corkboard and pin up images of who you want to become, how you want to look, where you want to live, how much money you want to make, et cetera and place it somewhere that makes you glance at it every day.

I Love Drills and Drills Love Me!

Pilots, police, marines, top athletes, actors and top business people all understand the power of drills. If you approach training drills with a lazy attitude, you will ingrain lazy habits. So whenever you're tempted to complain that you don't have the time and energy for training, get on your knees and shout, "I love drills and drills love me!" And remember, *you can't get the skills if you don't do the drills, and without better skills you can't get better results!*

Introvert vs. Extrovert

Most people think of introverts as antisocial and extroverts as those who love people. According to psychologists these definitions are a bit simplistic. They define an introvert as someone who likes to recharge their personal batteries by being alone, while an extrovert does so by being around other people. Which one are you?

If you do not know, it is time to find out. Not being aware of which one you are can cost you a great deal of time and distress. On the other hand, knowing how to recharge your batteries quickly can help you perform at higher and higher levels without burning out.

The worst thing you can ask a tired introverted person to do is be around a lot of people, and isolating an exhausted extrovert can put additional burden on them. You really can't put a price on self-awareness.

So which one are you?

Unpacking Belief Systems

I am a professional people-watcher. Over the years I have trained myself to notice the subtle differences among people and therefore I notice the little things most everyone else misses. It is both a skill and an enjoyable activity and it has proven invaluable to me.

Professional people-watching means using your eyes, ears, head, heart and gut when observing others. Learn to listen for the use of simple yet revealing "belief gateway" words and phrases such as "Is", "Am", "If", "Then", and "Are." I can assure you that when someone begins a sentence with things like "This is…", "I am…", "If you do that, then…" or "Those people are…", they are about to lead you straight to their belief systems.

Watch TV, listen to the radio and pay attention to your friends while watching for those psychological gateway phrases. Then compare them to that person's behaviors and traits. You will see some interesting patterns indeed.

In addition, filter what they are saying through your head, heart and gut to assess both the intention and the meaning of their communication.

Exercise: Watch (mainstream media and independent) news from various sources, and use your head, heart and gut to assess their real message. Then in order to develop a feel for key belief phrases for yourself, finish these sentences honestly and quickly:

- Sales is...
- I am...
- Money is...
- Profits are...
- This country is...
- If I work out every day then...
- If I spend less money, then...
- Salespeople are...
- Basketball players are...
- Paying taxes is...
- My home is...
- Eating healthfully is...
- The President / Prime Minister is...
- Smokers are...
- If I do the exercises in this book and reinforce them regularly then...

So let's bring what we just learned into a practical understanding. Our identity is what we believe about ourselves in various areas of our lives and it can be unpacked and changed by observing and modifying our internal and external language. In other words, we can develop an Unstoppable Attitude about ourselves simply by changing the structure of our language.

Say "I am,..." and complete that sentence with various personal scenarios, checking in with your head, heart and gut for congruency. Does what you say about yourself feel true?

Does your verbal self-description match up with your real identity or who you believe you are?

For example, I like to golf and for years I scored consistently in the low 80's to high 70's. I also like to play soccer and have played at a high level. I still enjoy both activities; however, if I say the words "I am a golfer" and/or "I am a soccer player," it just doesn't feel right, because the truth is "I am just a guy who likes to play golf and soccer." I don't and never have identified myself with being a golfer or a soccer player. Now if I say "I am an athlete" it feels true as I think, act and live that way, and it extends into my entire lifestyle.

The goal here is to understand that your identity is who you think you are and it drives your attitude toward everything you do. Keep in mind that you, your circumstances and your self-perception change over time. To play and watch soccer when I was younger was to participate in great quality games with the odd bad play; however as I get older and watch everyone get older with me, I realize that our pace of play have declined somewhat. My friends that identify themselves as soccer players just can't and probably never will come to grips with the fact that their level of play no longer fits their self-image. So they play with a level of intensity that I actually find silly and entertaining at times.

When I say, "I am a strategist, trainer and salesperson" every cell in my body knows that is true. Further, I am a sales trainer that sells and takes training! I am fully attached to and congruent with those two words and all their associated activities and outcomes. That means I approach sales training with an entirely different level of intensity than I do soccer or golf. Does this make sense?

The role of positive affirmations said with congruent language and tone is to change your beliefs about yourself, to change your identity. We always behave in accordance with who we really think we are.

When you say a direct statement about yourself with a strong tone and conviction over and over, your subconscious mind will start to identify with it and believe it. And when that happens you will start to act on it, for better or for worse.

Exercise: Review all your major activities, roles and goals and create some short direct statements that will improve your identity, increase your personal power and move you in the direction you want to go. Here are a few personal examples:

- **I am my industry's #1 Sales Trainer**
- **I am smart with my money**
- **I am a good parent**
- **If I'm consistent with my daily health and lifestyle habits I will be vibrant every day**
- **I love to create systems and processes that help people**
- **I'm grateful for every moment of every day**
- **I love my customers**
- **If somebody else can do it so can I**
- **I have the ability to create unlimited energy**
- **I will adapt to any changes.**

Affirmations use the principles of the Pygmalion effect, learned helplessness, goal-setting and subconscious mind direct statement programming to create convictions and visions that will start to move your mind and life in the direction you want.

As mentioned earlier, we cannot *not* communicate with ourselves; in fact, we are making statements (often negative ones) to ourselves all day long. So why not take a few minutes to create a menu of new, empowering statements that will take you where you want to go, redefining yourself and your life in ways you wish to see it? Then simply say them aloud with emotion each and every day.

It's not uncommon to see people sabotage their own success, usually because their identity does not match their underlying beliefs about who they really are. So we hit a level of success that our subconscious mind is uncomfortable with, then we start to change our behaviors in negative ways so that we slide back down to the level of person we really think we are. The great news is it's all self-made BS that can be changed!

Learned Helplessness

Exactly when and where did you start to accept and even expect all of your life's conditions and limitations? Things like how much money you are capable of making, how much debt is acceptable, your body shape, your position or station professionally, et cetera. The vast majority of us are not living the way in which we would have planned or hoped, oftentimes because we've had our aspirations beaten right out of us.

Of all the tens of thousands of people I have met, I can point to very few individuals who seem to have rejected most of the barriers and limitations that the rest of us blindly accept.

Perhaps the best illustration of learned helplessness is that of the elephant, a massive, strong and sentient being conditioned to obey its relatively tiny, unarmed, human master.

When a baby elephant is born it is separated from its mother and this creates insecurity and fear while starting the processes of containment and reliance. Then the elephant trainer begins to imprint themselves on the baby elephant as the provider of food and shelter, creating a feeling of dependence, whilst they tie the baby to a very large tree with a very heavy chain. The smart little elephant quickly realizes he can't pull the tree out of the ground with such a large chain around his leg and soon stops attempting to escape.

Over the next few months, using reinforcement, reward

and punishment, carrot and stick, the elephant starts to conform to the trainer's commands. As the elephant grows larger and stronger the trainer begins an inversion of its restraints, shifting to ever-smaller trees and lighter chains. Still, the elephant is conditioned to believe that whenever there is something around its neck or leg and attached to the ground, there is no point trying to escape. Then one day, people gather round to see the elephant being led around by a scrawny human holding nothing but a thin rope. This majestic creature could free itself in a moment, but it no longer *believes* it can. It has come to accept its limitations.

Occasionally you will hear of an elephant "losing its mind" and running away from their trainer, often taking out half a village with them and even gathering up any other elephants looking on. In reality the elephant and all witnessing elephants, regained consciousness and woke up from the controlling hypnotic trance they were placed under by the trainer. Unfortunately the elephants are usually killed, as their expanded levels of consciousness can never be contracted to where they were before. But learned helplessness only happens to elephants, right? Wrong. We are being trained in much the same way every single day. Once you start to wake up about yourself and the world around you, you will never see yourself and others or live the same way again.

Exercise: The following questions will help you realize—and break free of—some of the limitations that have been placed on you.

- What insecurities keep you from stepping outside your comfort zones?

- Who or what have you become dependent on and why?

- Why do you believe you can't reach higher?

- What would you do if you believed you couldn't fail?

- What has led you to accept your standard of living?

- Could you be just as happy with more or less?

- What rewards and punishments have been used on you throughout your lifetime to set your limitations?

- In what ways do the typical socialized fears of not being liked / loved or not being enough affect you?

- What limitations have you placed on yourself and why?

- How has the media, your friends, family, associates, culture or education affected how you think your life should be?

- Experiences, information and our imagination create, reinforce and challenge our beliefs and limitations. In what ways have your personal or world views changed over your life due to your experiences, information and imagination?

Welcome to the Life Game

As I have said a few times now, I believe the mark of an intelligent mind is the ability to entertain ANY thought without judging it; this starts with allowing people to discuss anything without judgement. I know I have provoked and offended people with the things I am willing to let people talk about, comments I will make or jokes I will tell. Unfortunately in this era of thin skins and political correctness, there are very few things you can say or allow someone to talk about that won't offend someone, somewhere. And I just won't live in that polarized and silenced way. If your intentions are good, you can talk with me about literally anything.

Several years ago, someone presented me with several "what-if" scenarios. At first it seemed just for fun but as I pondered these concepts I realized I found them profoundly interesting and any time a new perspective is taken new insights and directions can creep in...

Let's imagine that we are playing a virtual reality "Life Game", which can be best illustrated with life simulation games such as World of Warcraft or The Sims that are so popular nowadays. If you were to regularly play such games would you always choose to play the same player? Wouldn't you want to sometimes play a man, a woman, a child, the rich landlord, the poor tenant, the hunter, the gatherer, the king, the slave, the athlete, the winner and the loser just to try it out for some adventure and as a learning experience?

And what of others taking part in the game? Wouldn't you like them to alternately play with you and against you if only for the sake of competition and comparison? Wouldn't you invite some of your tougher competition to play against you once in a while? If you were no longer challenged and you knew you would win the game every single time you played, wouldn't you become bored and stop playing?

Even if you chose your roles, each interaction and game would be different because when using free will, everyone gets to make different choices, just to see how it would play out, while learning lots from each other along the way.

Have you ever noticed that when you're playing a very challenging game you become completely and totally immersed in your role, so much so that you forget you are just playing a game? Yet when your virtual player or avatar dies, you just reflect on that game and pick another character for the next. It is similar to the way pilots use flight simulators to grow their skills and have some safe fun.

Take a moment to play along with me. What if the real Game of Life worked the same way? What if at the end of each game when your player expired, all of your experiences, choices and why you chose them, were backed up onto some sort of hard drive, to be reviewed later by you and a Game Master for learning and coaching?

Now let's say that just before beginning this review the Game Master asks, "What did you do with all the potential you had in every area of your life? Of what caliber were your decisions? What were your intentions behind every decision? How much of your total potential did you actually use?" How would you answer? How would you feel watching that detailed review of your life file on that hard drive with the Game Master?

I find this metaphor presents some very interesting learnings. What if your life was nothing more than a broad set of learning experiences, with thousands of opportunities to grow up, wake up, improve yourself at the being level through so many experiences and contribute to the positive growth of others? What if you were your only competition in this game, with the sole goal of getting a little better in any way, every day?

Process this. Think about it. Meditate on it. This metaphor and concept could be a game changer, no pun intended.

Linear vs. Lateral Thinking

There are two dominant thinking styles.

When we are focused, single-minded, convicted and moving towards one goal, we are in a linear mindset. The upside of this thought process is great follow-through, the urge to complete a task coupled with the will to get it done. The downside is that when you are confronted with a problem while on that linear path and you just apply more linear pressure you will probably be met with frustration, while you throw more of the same at it, hoping your problem gives in for you. Linear thinkers can be skeptical and quite close-minded.

When we are unfocused, holding few convictions and not moving towards one goal, we are in a lateral mindset. The upside of this style of thinking is your ability to detach from just one methodology and urgency is reduced while you try different things. The downside is you may seek different options to the point of confusing yourself, never really apply any one strategy to its fullest potential, and keep skimming around the solutions without resolution. Lateral thinkers can be naïve and very open-minded.

Some people are either predominantly linear or lateral. That said, you could be skeptical in some areas of your life, and open-minded in others, so why not work on being open-minded and skeptical towards all things?

The most successful problem solvers and accomplishers of great things find a balance. They pursue a goal in a linear fashion, and when confronted with obstacles retreat slightly and attempt a different lateral solution. They move with purpose between linear and lateral, zigzagging their way toward their goal.

So, when you hit a wall, back up a bit, analyze the entire wall, find the best spot and method for your next approach, zigzag right or left, then go back at it again! Over and over until you find or create a way through it, beside it, under it or over it.

Logical Levels

There are six useful areas we can use to affect how we process and relate to any change we wish to make. These Six Logical Levels provide multi-pronged solutions, especially when you build in measurable feedback at each level to let you know whether your plan is working. Always judge by results, and if you're not getting the results you want simply investigate, stay flexible and try something else. The following is an elegant and effective NLP (Neuro Linguistic Programming) exercise to map out your goals.

Exercise: Grab seven pieces of paper and a pen. Go ahead and get them, I can wait. Ready...? On the top of the first sheet of paper, write down a precise and measurable goal, for example, "Pay off $50,000 of debt." Please don't just write down, "Pay Off Debt"—make sure to include the actual dollar amount, so you can easily check for feedback and evidence of your progress as you move toward or away from that exact goal.

On the remaining six pieces of paper, write the words "ENVIRONMENT/SURROUNDINGS"; "BEHAVIORS/ ACTIVITIES"; "STRATEGIES/SKILLS"; "BELIEFS/ VALUES"; "IDENTITY/ME"; and "PURPOSE/ MISSION". Place the piece of paper with your goal on the ground, then step backward and start to place the other six areas one pace apart, with ENVIRONMENT/

SURROUNDINGS at the bottom and PURPOSE/ MISSION at the top, closest to the goal.

Now we will tackle the levels one at a time. Starting at the bottom level, you will go through the questions below. Read each question aloud, then close your eyes and think about your answer. After a minute or so, write down whatever came to you, then step up to the next level and repeat the process. Repeat this until you have gone through them all.

1. ENVIRONMENT/SURROUNDINGS

Slowly review your entire day, and all your physical surroundings, from the time you wake up until the time you go to bed again. What are some things within and around your environment and surroundings that you could add, change or delete to make the attainment of or focus on, this goal easier? Where could you place reminders and support items? How or what could you place in your environment to further assist you with this goal? Your surroundings also pertain to the people around you. Who supports you, who doesn't? Who can you learn from, who are your good and bad examples, who should you avoid and who should you spend more time with throughout your day?

2. BEHAVIORS/ACTIVITIES

Again, review a typical day from start to finish. We do things every day that take us away from or move us toward our goals. What can you modify, do more of, do less of, what should you start or stop doing to make the attainment of this goal easier? What specific behaviors, in what situations, need to be addressed? Now mentally rehearse doing the things you know you need to do!

3. STRATEGIES/SKILLS

What skills do you need to master? What do you need to learn more about? What books, courses, websites, mentors, et cetera should you research to help you hit this goal? What strategies would you have to employ or deploy to help with the attainment of this goal?

4. BELIEFS/VALUES

What do you believe regarding your ability to hit this goal? What do you believe and how do you feel about other people that have attained similar goals? What is your emotional reaction to the things you need to do and the people you need to align yourself with to help you get this goal? What do you believe and value that is in alignment with your goals? And what is in conflict with your goals? What beliefs do you need to adopt or change, and what values do you need to shift to make the attainment of this goal easier?

5. IDENTITY/ME

Who are you, really? What do you stand for? What sort of person were you in the past and what sort of person do you have to become in the future in order to hit your goal? How do you see yourself? Someone somewhere has hit and will hit a similar goal, so why can't it be you? What did they have to become to hit their goal?

6. PURPOSE/MISSION

Do you feel aligned with a bigger purpose, something that uplifts and empowers yourself and others? In what ways will hitting this goal help you, those nearest to you, your community, or even the world?

As you address these six logical levels your stress levels will fall, your clarity will rise and your results will follow. Like everything else in this book, I know this because I've done it and continue to do so on a regular basis.

The Eight Pillars of Well-Being

Reader, if you ask anyone who has attended my trainings or read my books they'll tell you I am a big believer in process, checklists and acronyms. I also believe there is generally no quick fix for bigger issues and that a multi-pronged approach is always best.

Below is a checklist focused on what I consider to be the "Eight Pillars of Well Being." It serves as a great guideline for the areas you need to be aware of and working on when it comes to well-being. Together, they spell a weird word "MMEEENRS," which can be used as a checklist to gauge your overall sense of well-being or lack thereof. I can tell you from experience, when you start to improve multiple areas in small ways the incremental benefits start stacking up and you begin to notice subtle and obvious changes to your Unstoppable Attitude, as well as both your achievement and fulfillment levels! Every strategy in this book falls under one or more of the **MMEEENRS.**

Exercise: If you want to move toward more vitality and away from anything that may be ailing you, just go down this list, reflect on each area and be sure you are doing multiple things to improve them. A problem or imbalance in any area can affect any or all of the other areas.

M—Mechanical (the condition of our organs, neuromuscular and skeletal structures affects how we function, think and feel, so do things that improve your mechanics such as stretching, massage, yoga, lifting weights, chiropractic, et cetera.)

M—Mental (pay attention to your dominant thought processes, views, information, beliefs, values, intentions, mindfulness, concentration, ANTs, et cetera and work on changing them in the direction you want.)

E—Energetic (life uses electricity so assess and adjust your polarity and energy flows using acupuncture, reiki, Kirlian photography, EFT, et cetera.)

E—Emotional (what is your repetitive dominant feelings, reactions, desires, repulsions, Collectives, et cetera and if you need to, work on adjusting them.)

E—Environmental (do the physical items around your home, work, car and common environments support you? If not, change them.)

N—Nutrition (the quantity and quality of your nutrition and hydration may need some attention.)

R—Relationships (review the quantity and quality of your primary relationships as well as any past relationships that may be still affecting you.)

S—Spiritual (review your connection to a Higher Source, whatever that means for you; it also includes community giving, feeling you are contributing to a greater good, et cetera.)

The examples I used above in each area of MMEEENRS is far from exhaustive; in fact there are probably hundreds of different ways to improve and maintain each area, depending on your personal interests and culture. The important point here is to make you aware of what the areas are, and then you can research the ways to improve them that make sense to you. In the meantime, ask yourself: What areas am I ignoring? What areas am I paying too much attention to? What things need to be added, changed or deleted in my regular focus and activities to help support my gaps and weak links? As you explore and become more curious, you will find the list is always changing. Mine certainly does.

I refer to this list often; in fact, it's one of the things on my home screen of my smartphone, so I glance at it all the time and reflect on how I am doing in these areas. (The other screen savers on my phone are a picture of myself when I was two years old, and whenever I look at it I ask myself, "How am I treating this little guy and am I being good to him?" as well as my wealth checklist "PAASSCDTT", which you can learn more about in my book *Unstoppable Money*.)

Ninety-Nine Percent Off-Course

Do you ever feel like you are lost or off course?

I've read that an airplane is technically off course the vast majority of the time, sometimes up to 99% of the flight! In big and small ways it is constantly being pulled, pushed, up, down, to the left or to the right. Yet because it knows exactly where it started, keeps a keen fix on where it wants to go and makes constant adjustments along the way, it arrives at the desired location.

What an elegant analogy for life. We are being dragged or nudged off course continually but if we are self-aware, have written goals and refer to them daily, be patient and continue making adjustments, we can arrive anywhere we wish to go!

Muscles of the Mind

Exercise: Fold or cross your arms in front of you. Now try to fold them in exactly the opposite way. Not easy, right? Did you notice how quickly and comfortably your first habitual arm fold was to do? I've seen some people in my seminars unable to fold their arms perfectly opposite to their natural fold even after minutes of trying.

This is muscle memory, and it is not just a cute term but a biological reality. We have neurons spread throughout our body, and as mentioned earlier with the highest concentration of neurons in our brain, our heart and our gut, so it just makes sense that these are our three dominant decision-making centers.

A lot of study has gone into how habits are formed and broken. The dominant conclusions are that habits are formed through repetition, the seeking of pleasure or the avoidance of pain, and our number-one need: survival.

Think of muscle memory and neural pathways as chemical and electrical highways that have been laid down throughout your body to allow you to easily (sometimes unconsciously) replicate actions, behaviors, gain pleasure, avoid pain and extend our survival, almost like triggers, switches and programs do in machines. Which one of these scenarios would you say results in the quickest programming of a behavior for most people:

1. Exposure to something that created pain (thereby programming an avoidance to anything that resembles that in the future and perhaps installing a Collective);

2. Exposure to something that led to pleasure (so you seek out that or similar behaviors to gain the pleasure again); or

3. Repeating a thought or action hundreds of times (so it becomes a habit).

For most of us, the answer is number one, as we are built to avoid pain as a survival mechanism.

Understanding this, how can you program yourself for more success and less failure?

Exercise: Pick a habit you are trying to change, close your eyes, and imagine everything and anything that could go wrong now, and in the future, as a result of not changing. Exaggerate all the implications in every area you can imagine: health, wealth, happiness, how others relate to you, your longevity, productivity, image, social status and future opportunities. Then write down all those possible negative outcomes and implications of not changing and fully associate pain with them in any analytical or emotional ways you can. What you will probably find is that you are now getting some serious leverage on yourself and motivation (motive to action) on what and why you need to change.

If you burn your hand on an imaginary stove over and over, when the real stove presents itself, you won't need any coaching on why you should not touch it.

You can goal set to seek pleasure or avoid pain, but pain is associated with the possibility of threatening our survival, so it's hard wired into us and you can use your "moving away from instincts" to manage your habits. For the most part I maintain good lifestyle habits because I don't want to get sick, good money habits as I don't want to be poor and use the techniques in this book on myself as I don't want to be unhappy or unproductive. Remember, if you remove the causes of failure what you have left over is more success. But first you have to understand and associate with real or perceived failures.

Once your neural pathways (habits) are set, these habits create your life, so start to lay them down with intention and attention.

The Power of a Nose

How much better do you have to be than your competition?

When it comes to things such as horse racing or Olympic sprinting, the winner of the race is often recorded with a photo finish, sometimes only millimeters ahead of second place. It may not be a fair or accurate representation of talent and skill, but being just a nose ahead can be the difference between being recorded in history forever and forgotten almost instantly.

If a horse wins by a nose is it really that much better than the horse in second place? What gave it that nose? Was it training, technique, genes, nutrition, hydration, breathing, body proportions, the jockey, mentality, lack of injuries or its sleep the night before? Hard to tell and it doesn't really matter, because she is now the champion.

Just like doubling a penny every day for thirty days builds into over $5,000,000, if you strive to be just a nose better each day in one year you will be 365 noses ahead of where you are today and the compound effects of that could be staggering!

Exercise: Each day, ask yourself, "What can I improve today to make myself just a little better than I was yesterday, in any way?"

Pain vs Pleasure

Which scenario would make you act on first, the possibility of losing $100,000 or of making $100,000? Do you love to win or do you hate to lose? Which is a bigger motivator for you? Really think that through as it's an important distinction you need to be aware of.

The amount of money in either scenario is the same, but how you feel about it is probably very different.

If you're more inspired by the idea of making $100,000, you love to win and are probably a eustress and endorphin seeker who is motivated by chasing higher highs.

If you're more disturbed by the thought of losing $100,000, you hate to lose and are likely a distress and cortisol avoider who will be motivated more by avoiding lower lows.

If both are equally motivating, you are an unusually competitive person.

Exercise: Think of a goal you are seeking and imagine it with feeling, as being real now. If you love to win, imagine what it would be like to hit that goal; if you hate to lose, imagine what it would be like for you not to hit it, or maybe even for it to be taken away from you. Figure out which is more inspiring for you and fully associate with it.

We either act on our desire to seek pleasure or our need to avoid pain, but most of us don't act on them in equal proportions. Knowing which one is your "master system" is a key to being able to motivate yourself more effectively and will explain a lot of your past behavior as well as predict your future actions.

Step Back from the Tribe

Most of us associate the term "peer pressure" with the ways in which children try to exert influence over each other in order to get them to behave in certain ways. Truth is, peer pressure and tribal influence are powerful forces at any age.

As I mentioned earlier, from birth we are bombarded with ideas about how we should behave, how much money we should make, what we should look like, what kind of habits we should have, et cetera. These ideas often become the expectations for our lives.

Around the age of twenty-five I made a conscious decision to change my habits around my money, my health, my happiness and my work. I was aware that I had adopted my habits in those areas from my culture, family and friends, and although I loved them I didn't want my life to be like theirs in many ways.

What I quickly realized was that most people really don't want to see you change or improve in any significant way. They are comfortable with you in the way things are and can become threatened when you start to change. This is true even of your closest family and friends and this fact can make it difficult to keep up positive momentum. So you may often find yourself sliding back into your old habits, just to avoid making waves.

When I found out that many top performers are to some extent loners for this reason, I decided to slightly back away from my peer group. I began spending much of my personal time alone so I could study and take on new ways of thinking and behaving without the influence of others. I found new peer groups and role models that more closely matched who I wanted to become in books, audio courses, mentors, workshops and websites. I found in those circles there was a different kind of peer pressure because those peers were more concerned with bringing others up, rather than keeping people down. The fun part is that as I continue to grow, I need to (and do) find new "peers" and "teachers" that I want to associate with and emulate.

I also learned early on to goal set privately. I would prefer to hear, "How did you do that?" once the goal is obtained than, "Why do you want to do that?" or worse, "You can't do that!" before I even start. Believe me when I say you don't really know who your friends are until you start doing well. At first it's disheartening and disappointing, to find your co-workers, friends and even family acting differently around you when you start making positive changes to your life and getting better results. In addition, if any of those changes involve going against their deep-seated cultural or spiritual beliefs, buckle up, because that ride will be bumpy!

There's an old saying: "Don't walk with the wicked or the stupid, lest you become them." It may sound overly dramatic, but beware the strong pull of your social circles and how they try to draw you in whatever direction they are headed. Question is, are they headed where you want to go?

People-People vs. Activity People

Question: When you are bored or looking for something to do, do you go to people or do you go to your to-do list? If you asked your friends, what would they say about you? Do you tend to seek out tasks or entertainment with others.

We need relationships, but we also need to get things done. Studies of tens of thousands of top business professionals have determined that most top-in-class people are activity seekers, or activity people. They are always focused on their to-dos, creating and completing new tasks, and one of those tasks is networking with people!

The previous chapter discussed peer groups and peer pressure. Think about it, if you're constantly seeking the entertainment and attention of others you will very likely be influenced by their habits and behaviors, which is fine, unless you have different aspirations than them. When I was young I exposed myself to many different jobs and a great mantra I learned working at McDonald's in high school was "If you have time to lean, you have time to clean!" In other words, stay productive! The saying was not "If you have time to lean, you have time to hang out and just hope something good happens with your buddies!"

By focusing on your task list, which may even include expanding productive peer groups and staying connected with your friends, you are a purpose-driven builder of the foundations of your life and business. Remember what you do in between clients is as important as what you do when you are with them.

Three Causes of Suffering

Many artists have said that they could see the final sculpture or masterpiece hidden in the block of wood or stone and that all they did was remove all the material that was covering it up. In much the same way I truly believe we are born to be healthy, happy and successful but we are surrounded with all sorts of stuff that hinders our innate potential to have it all.

Each day I ask myself several directed questions. For example, one of my daily questions is, "How do I want my day to be?" And I can tell you that neither I nor any of my students have ever answered with, "Lousy, frustrating or crappy." Why? Because our true nature is to be exceptional! However, if you're not vigilant life will get in the way and cover up your natural potential. When you remove the most common causes of suffering, what you are left with is space for your true positive essence to blossom.

Thousands of years of philosophical studies of human behavior has shown that most suffering has three main causes:

1. Clinging. I work hard to keep my health, wealth, relationships and happiness, but everything, and I mean everything, is impermanent. Let things go, let change happen, let people go, let youth go, do not attach to anything, material or otherwise. One day everything we hold near and dear will disappear. Believe it or not,

once you truly own this concept, the levels of joy and appreciation you experience in even the most mundane things becomes hard to describe because you realize how precious every moment is. It also reduces anxiety (a fear of what may happen), because a large part of our distress stems from the impossible and illogical need to hold on to impermanent things. This doesn't mean you become flippant or detached from everything, it just means you train yourself to stop emotionally clinging to anything and anyone.

Exercise: Look at every person, place and thing around you and imagine them all in the future as the dust and dirt it logically will eventually become. Do this for one second, one minute, one hour or an entire day. You will emerge from this exercise incredibly grateful for every moment and every thing in your life. Do this often, perhaps daily.

2. Craving. I find that reducing and eliminating clinging automatically stops most of my cravings, as it becomes glaringly obvious that craving impermanent things is illogical. It is important here to make the distinction between craving and seeking. While I am seeking improvement in many different areas of my personal and professional life, I am careful not to emotionally crave them. Many terrible emotions such as jealousy, depression, obsessiveness, addictions, impulsiveness and the like are all related to craving and clinging to things. Be aware that by reducing your clinging and craving, you will not diminish your drive

to succeed or improve. What it will do is strip away any negative emotions or reactions that are caused by constantly grasping at things you do not have now or perhaps will never have and reduce clinging to them once you obtain them.

Exercise: Review your and other people's achievements, goals and desires assessing the quality of emotion you have towards them. If you find any of the above types of undesirable emotional associations with them, remind yourself of how everything and everyone eventually become dust and dirt. This shift in perspective will allow you to seek but not crave.

3. Ignorance. Not understanding the gross and subtle negative effects that clinging and craving can cause on your life and the lives of others is an obvious cause of suffering. So in many ways clinging, craving and ignorance are tightly connected. Lack of information and knowledge creates lack of power and choice. (As a side note, this is essentially why lying is considered immoral, as it takes away the other person's power and choice in that situation.) If you are trying to move in a certain direction but don't have the best tools (i.e. knowledge) to get the job done, you will be met with unnecessary delays. This is why daily skills-building, studying things outside your normal scope of thinking, finding a mentor and staying open-minded but skeptical are so crucial. Many of our frustrations are actually rooted in ignorance; as we want things to be different than they are, but we may not really have a

full understanding of why things are the way they are. This needs to be balanced with our need for certainty, and accept the fact that we will never really have all the answers to everything. If we can live without fear and ego and realize we don't and can't know everything, we can humbly go about the task of continual study and improvement.

Exercise: Think of one thing that is a source of suffering in your life, and place its cause under one or more of the three areas above. Next, try it with your closest friend. Then, when you can detach from the emotion of your suffering by attaching to the actual source of your suffering from one of the areas above, start to analyze any and all aspects of your life in this same way, and continue to do so as needed for the rest of your life. You may find it helpful to do this exercise with your eyes closed. Create a habit of scanning all aspects of your life looking for the causes of your suffering, just like a computer scans it's systems looking for a virus.

A Feast for the Senses

Neuro-linguistic Programming (NLP) studies and demonstrates how we use our senses to gather, store, associate and recall information.

The best way to remember these five senses is with the acronym VAKOG, which stands for visual (sight), auditory (sounds), kinesthetic (touch), olfactory (smell) and gustatory (taste). And because we both externally gather and internally represent information about our world using these five senses, NLP makes a clear distinction between the world around us (objective external) and how we interpret it (subjective internal). A common NLP phrase is that the map (our interpretations) does not equal the territory (the way the world is). What's interesting about this is that if you change your internal map, you can change your reactions to and actions in, your external world.

Reader, for most of us, the primary method of information recall is internal visual images. If I asked you to remember exactly what you had for dinner last night, you will most likely pull up an image. Doesn't it stand to reason that changing your attraction, desire, drive, dislike or repulsion for people, places, activities and behaviors could be as easy as changing how you recall the image of it? Could you really reprogram yourself to be more or less interested, engaged, fearful, excited and happy about things, just by changing how your brain stores these things? Absolutely. Try it for yourself, on yourself, with anything you wish, then be sure to train your brain repetitively with these new representations. With practice, you will surprise yourself as to how effective and fast this can be. Talk about speed therapy!

Exercise: You're going to need some help with this one. Get someone to read the following to you whilst you sit down, close your eyes and relax. "Think of anything or anyone you really like, are attracted to, don't like or are repulsed by. Put up your right hand when you have an image of one of these in your mind. Note the intensity of your feelings toward it. Okay, now let's play internal emotional movie director and begin slowly making changes to the sub-modalities, or ways you represent this image to yourself.

"Make it very vibrant in color, make it a massive panorama you are immersed in, accentuate any tastes or smells and turn up any sounds that may be present, bring it closer and closer so you are zoomed right up to the parts that make you feel the best, then take that image and make it crystal-clear and focused. Now take a deep breath and breathe in all the best parts of that image emotionally and physically. Take note of how you feel right now about it. Have your feelings intensified since we made the sub-modality changes?" I would be willing to bet yes.

Open your eyes, then close them again.

"Now bring the original image back up, before the adjustments. Put up your right hand when you have the original image in your mind. Okay, let's play emotional mental movie director again and slowly make some changes to the image you are holding in your mind. Make it black and white, put a sterile white frame around it so it looks like an old Polaroid picture, shut off any tastes or smells, replace all sounds with the sound of very quiet radio static, push the image further, further and further away until it's barely the size of a small postage stamp and then take the image and make it blurry and out of focus. Take note of how you feel right now. Have your feelings lessened since we made the sub-modality changes?" You will probably find that they have.

So what is the takeaway here? Bring into your conscious attention, not just what you think about, but HOW you represent what you think about. And, using what you just learned here, practice changing how you feel about things by changing how you internally represent them. When helping someone feel differently about things in their lives by reading the above sub-modality changes to them, you don't need to know what they are working on or why, and in this way it is considered to be context-free therapy, as the person being coached doesn't need to tell their coach any personal information about the situation. Using this "change technology" does not require any will power as you are simply changing HOW you internally represent it, and thereby changing   WHAT your reaction to it is. Repetitive conditioning of the new "image" will install it and change your feelings about it forever.

Placebo

The "placebo effect" is a term coined to describe how our thoughts and beliefs manifest into real world outcomes with measurable results. While this can be applied to any area of life, it has been most commonly associated with medicine and health. Whenever a drug company is about to launch a new medication, they are supposed to conduct years of studies, which should include trial groups. Some of these groups are given the actual drug, while others are given a placebo, or a sugar and salt pill. The participants do not know what group they belong to, however, all of them are given the same information about the supposed benefits of the "medication". The results of these tests have been amazing, with about one-third of the placebo group getting the full benefits of the medication. In simple terms, the mere belief that they are taking a pill that will benefit them drives their result. This may sound crazy, but for this reason I always "verbally instruct" my supplements about what they are supposed to be doing for me when I take them.

Perhaps even more amazing are surgical placebo studies. In one such study, people with knee injuries were told about a surgical procedure that would heal them. However, after all the patients were given anesthesia, only some of them underwent the actual surgery. The others received only a small, shallow incision. When they woke up they were all told they'd had the real surgery and that it was a success! As with the pills in the previous study, about one-third of the patients given the placebo surgery experienced a miraculous healing.

The power of our minds to affect our physical world is truly astounding. In a similar way this may be why we utilize a higher percentage of our foods nutrients if we give grace and gratitude to our nutrition before ingesting it. This effect is also why some interventionists are trained to wear their "greens, white coats, collars, feathers, face paint or special jewelry" when consulting with us, as the mere sight of that clothing causes us to associate them with authority and special knowledge, instilling in us the belief that what they say is fact, thereby triggering the placebo effect and increasing the odds of the desired results.

The "nocebo" effect is the exact same phenomenon but in reverse. In other words people experience negative effects, in the same proportions, driven only by their minds. So a person who believes in voodoo will be more negatively affected than one who doesn't believe in it.

Years ago, my former business partner and good friend Terry was diagnosed with lung cancer. He was just thirty-six at the time, I was 24 and was told he would be lucky to see his next birthday. Seemingly fine beforehand, from the moment he received that timeline from the white coats, his health began to deteriorate rapidly. I used to wonder what would have happened if he was never told he had it or if he rejected their diagnosis. Unbelievably, he passed away on his birthday. I saw the exact same thing happen with my father. Perhaps this is all coincidence, perhaps not.

It is therefore imperative that you constantly reinforce the positive impact and benefits you expect to receive from everything you do, participate in, surround yourself with and ingest. And guard your mind vigilantly against any disempowering or dangerous beliefs.

You can apply the placebo effect to anything in your life. In fact, this may be what Napoleon Hill meant when he said, "Conceive it, Believe it, Achieve it." By the same token, be very careful what ideas you are buying and from who. This is another reason why I don't watch TV or listen to the news, as I am not interested in buying the fear-based controlled agenda most News Actors try to sell us, day after day.

Dead Man Walking

How many car accidents are caused by someone not paying attention? How many opportunities are missed, sales and profits are lost or friendships are harmed by not paying attention?

There used to be a popular military term called "dead man walking." It was a label given to soldiers for their first thirty days of active combat and their last thirty days after they were notified that they were going home. Why? When they first arrived into combat, their minds and hearts were often still at home and missing their families, so they were not paying attention to their surroundings as closely as they should be. When they got their thirty-day notice that they were being sent home their minds and hearts left before they did so again they were not focused on their situation. Statistically those two periods had the highest death rates during their terms of service. Because of this, the first month and last month of service were very dangerous times for them and anyone near them. It was not unusual for them to be avoided by others or isolated during those periods.

While not as dangerous, we can apply the same rule about paying attention to civilian life. Have you ever heard the saying, "Go to work to work"? To do this you must first learn to leave your home at home! Dragging negativity into work from your personal life or wishing you were at home with your lovely family while you are at work can cost you enormously in terms of poor focus, missed opportunities and lost profits.

If you're a salesperson you know that people today have shorter attention spans and a sea of distractions, so continual focus by either the seller or the buyer is a rarity. Most customers are the most focused when they first meet us. They size us up, feel our energy and judge us. They may lose some focus during the sales process but they are extremely tuned in during the close. These are your "dead man walking" periods. You need to be extremely aware and tight with your personal presentation and process when you first meet the customer and when you're wrapping things up at the end. Beware, sales, like planes, tend to crash at take-off and landing.

It is also vital to have your customer with you as much as possible, within earshot or in your peripheral vision, so you can control their experience. Paying attention in this way will allow you to pick up hints and tips about their concerns and preferences.

So whether on the phone or in person, pay attention to the little differences that can make the big differences and you will make less mistakes and have much more success overall.

The Push-Push

Exercise: Get two people to face each other with the left hand of one pressed to the right hand of the other, palm to palm and fingertip to fingertip. Then say "On the count of three I want the person with their right hand up to push! 1, 2, 3 … Push! Push! Push!"

Notice what happens. The left-handed person instinctively pushes against the right-handed person without being instructed to do so. After doing this with several thousand people, I can say I've only seen a couple of left hands drop or get out of the way of the pushy right-handed person.

Why? People do not like to be pushed into accepting something, even if that something may be good for them.

In life you are either selling or being sold something by someone all the time. Real selling is about being persuasive, not pushy.

Pygmalion Effect

Decades ago there were experiments in which schoolteachers and their classes were divided into two separate groups.

The first group was told that their class was composed of bad students, behavioral issues, learning challenges, bad families and that it was obviously going to be a tough year.

The other group of teachers were told that they had a group of great, eager, open-minded students with supportive families. This random experiment was repeated dozens of times with different groups of teachers in different school systems and different students.

What was the outcome? On average those told they had bad students had bad results, and those told they had good students had good results. What the teachers didn't know, until the school year ended, was that each class was just a normal group of kids with the usual varying work ethic, attitude and talent.

What the results of these studies clearly concluded was that the teachers belief about the students expected behavior (good or bad) is what the students became. The students became what the teacher projected onto them.

What are you projecting onto your people with your thoughts, language and body language? Your children? Family? Friends? Customers? People often become what we expect them to be. Maybe our world is really a reflection of our expectations about who we are and how we think, act and believe, and by changing those projections we can change our world.

Begin to attach and project better attitudes, beliefs and expectations onto others. Treat them exactly how you would like them to become, as if they were already those people. The Pygmalion Effect is powerful and you can use it to better your life and those around you.

Exercise: Review all the people you interact with during a typical day and ask yourself, "Am I verbally or non-verbally influencing them in any negative ways that I am not aware of and how is this affecting my relationship with them or the utilization of their own future potential?"

Then start to project a desired behavior onto someone for some time, with absolute congruency, that they are already the way you want them to be and observe what starts to happen.

RAS

Have you ever noticed that when you buy a new car you suddenly start to notice that same make and model everywhere? If you like to exercise I bet you know where most of the fitness facilities are in your area. If you are not interested in golf you probably don't know where the golf courses are. Why?

Our Reticular Activating System (RAS) is a miraculous little piece of psychology and biology that watches out for things that are of potential interest to us, even without our conscious awareness!

If you were dropped into the middle of a vast forest or desert, the first things you would instinctively look for are water and shelter. Those two items are hardwired into your RAS for survival. Golfers notice where all the golf courses are, swimmers notice where the swimming pools are and cooks can find the kitchens in the same way.

Depending on what interests you, what you value or what your goals are, your RAS will be looking for such items to make sure you get what you want in life as easily and readily as possible. In an odd way this is why some men wear mirrored glasses to the beach. They know they won't be able to control where their eyes go, so their mirrored sunglasses provide them some sense of privacy, or so they think (dudes, women are on to you, so take them off and show some discipline!).

How do you program your RAS? Change your values, interests and goals. Remember your energy flows where your focus goes and your RAS seeks whatever you really want to find, either good or bad. So be careful what you give your energy, interest, values, goals and attention to.

Exercise: Activate your RAS and point it in any direction you wish by holding onto a thought with emotional intensity frequently and condition this thought regularly.

Do you see how intense goal setting, the Pygmalion Effect, placebos and so many other technologies overlap and will redirect your mind and life if applied?!

Releasing People

Are there some people you just wish you could distance yourself from? Maybe not forget entirely but perhaps just reduce or eliminate their emotional or psychological influence on you?

Exercise: Have someone read this to you: "Close your eyes, and imagine you and this person connected by bands or ropes, whatever color they are or whatever thickness they are in your mind's eye is right for you. Now have them float away, away, away, getting smaller and smaller, while you feel the connections become weaker and you say, over and over, "Everyone is free and it feels great." Now imagine a pair of large scissors coming into view and floating over to the ropes and bands, then cutting them. The ropes, bands and attachments drift off, floating so far into the distance you can barely make out the details. Notice how great it feels to be so far removed from them. As they drift off unharmed wish them well, lower the sounds, make the image black and white, turn your back to them, walk away and take a deep breath as you open your eyes."

Repeat this exercise until you feel the effects of this person diminish or disappear.

Note: there are five concepts in this book that are great for releasing other people's influence over you: Funny Fruit or

Vegetable, Sub-modality Changes, EFT, Relationship Solutions and Releasing People. You may even want to stack them all together.

EFT

Most of us have some emotional or psychological baggage we would like to leave at the curb or a nagging physical issue that we would like to rid ourselves of. Thankfully there are methods such as the Emotional Freedom Technique (EFT) that can help us do just that.

In my never-ending, open-minded but very skeptical journey to find new modalities to help myself and others I came across a well studied and very popular method to help people overcome almost an unlimited assortment of disorders, diseases, depression and difficulties. Like everything I write about, talk about, teach and do, I always go first. So I used EFT on myself, my friends, family and clients and the results were astounding.

I know we sometimes think our problems are pervasive, permanent and persistent. But I am telling you firsthand, I have seen a vast array of emotional, physical, psychological and even spiritual obstacles be massively reduced or eliminated in a matter of minutes right before my eyes, never to return. Years and years of failed therapy and accumulated traumas can vanish in minutes. This technique is very well studied and the results well documented and if you're open-minded and skeptical like me, you will need to check it out for yourself.

I have personally helped many people with things like fear of rejection/commitment/success/failure; phobias of isolation/spiders/relationships/heights/water/flying, past traumas with parents/siblings/spouses/war/rape/physical pains from bad backs/carpal tunnel/knees/headaches/migraines. There is no end to who and what can benefit from this rapid reset of your nervous system. As they say, you can try it on everything!

If you could possibly gain benefit in so many areas almost instantly, for no or little money and without drugs, why not try it?

There is probably an EFT practitioner near you, and you can learn how to do it online if you wish.

Relationship Solutions

A 2500 year old practice suggests that the four pillars of having quality relationships with imperfect beings such as ourselves and others are:

- Compassion
- Tolerance
- Patience
- Wisdom

On a daily basis I think of people, organizations and situations I find especially trying and I project on them, and myself, more and more of those four qualities.

I have found the quality, quantity and longevity of all my professional and personal interactions have improved substantially because of this easy exercise, as well as reducing my distress levels.

Remember, for things to change for you, things have to change about you. When you consider and project more compassion, tolerance, patience and wisdom on and for the world around you, you gain more of these things for yourself.

Exercise: Think of someone that is causing you distress. Now, hold them in your mind, take deep slow breaths and say, "Compassion, Tolerance, Patience and Wisdom," in a compassionate, tolerant, patient and wise tone, projecting those qualities and emotions on them, over and over, for whatever reasons they or you may need it.

Rearview Mirror

Your car has a large front windshield and relatively smaller rearview mirror for a reason. It's more important to keep your eyes fixed on where you are going than to focus on where you have been.

Exercise: Really try to imagine that your rearview mirror is the size of your front windshield, and your windshield is cut into that huge rear-view mirror. In other words, flipping your biggest visual cues onto where you have been, and your smallest visual cues onto where you are going. Now really picture what it would be like driving your car if it was equipped this way! How confusing would this be! Driving forward while mostly referencing where you have been would be disorienting, distressing and a real danger to yourself and others.

Here's another example—imagine you have a movie playing, looping over and over, that displays all the car accidents and near-misses you've ever had and that you watched that movie several times a day, or perhaps had it playing in your bedroom while you were sleeping. Might you become insecure and even paranoid about your driving skills? Isn't this what's going on when you single out from your past your mistakes, failures and challenges and play them over and over in your head?

As silly as this sounds this is how many people live their entire lives. They continually talk about the problems in their past, with clarity, conviction and emotion. Constantly mulling over some lousy version of what they think happened. Notice that when you try to talk to some people about how they can design their tomorrow, they often look at you as if you have three heads!

Newspapers and the nightly news are built to report, keep us focused on, and concerned about, our (negative) pasts. This is another reason why I don't watch the news. By the time the ink in the newspaper dries the entire situation could have changed. Live television reporters rarely do a 360-degree camera shot to show us what's really happening all around the scene. They only show us the slice they want us to focus on. All of this trains our brains to narrow the scope of our consideration even further and encourages us to look back on our timelines, rather than forward. When neurons wire together they fire together, even concerning things like our habitual timeline references.

Your future does not equal your past unless you choose to live there and there are no such things as mistakes, just learning experiences.

Exercise: For one week, talk only about the present and the future. Every time you talk about something in the past make yourself do one push up, sit up or squat.

Cognitive Dissonance

It has long been believed that the left side of the brain is involved primarily with logic and numbers while the right side is involved with relationships and spacial interactions.

If you are a salesperson, are you stronger with the people part of the sale (right brain) or the transactional part of the sale (left brain)? What would happen to your sales and income if you became equally strong with both?

There are many exercises and games you can Google, Bing or YouTube that are designed to increase the dexterity and depth of either your right or left brain. Think of it as going to a gym for the mind.

Let's move on to cognitive dissonance, which occurs when new, factual information contradicts what we have believed to be true. Our need for certainty may drive us to retreat into our old beliefs, ignoring the new information because to retrain and re-educate ourselves could simply be too much to handle. Most beliefs don't stand alone but are entangled and involved with many other beliefs, so to shed or change just one belief could have a domino effect on countless others. Can you see how our beliefs can box us in and keep us from growing?

Here is a rather odd tidbit I learned through my research: some people are living very productive and normal lives and have no brain at all! True story. I don't pretend to understand this, but it's a fact. Research terms like, "Do we even need a brain?" and "Does consciousness need a brain?" as well as the websites of McGill University and the University of West Virginia. Get ready! I think the fact that high IQ brainless individuals exist and live perfectly healthy and normal lives creates cognitive dissonance with much of the medical and psychological community, so it never gets the discussion or attention it deserves. Some people without brains are lawyers and doctors! So where is there legal and medical knowledge stored if they don't have a brain?

Here's another very different example that may cause cognitive dissonance: did you know that the standard concept of how protons and neutrons spin around an electron (so it sort of looks like a mini solar system) has actually never been observed? It's only a theory! In fact, it is now being taught in a way that makes it look more like a cloud.

Also, as a child I had to recite the words "the gospels according to Matthew, Mark, Luke and John" hundreds of times, but I never thought to ask the question "who wrote the gospels and when?"

How many things have we been taught or told as objective facts are actually just subjective concepts? I am not making any judgements about the validity of any beliefs of any kind! I am just stating a fact that we often don't question or challenge them.

In our pursuits of wealth, health and happiness we are often faced with new facts that are in direct conflict with what we first believed. Being able to recognize and deal with this conflict in an intelligent and detached way is fundamental to improving yourself.

I strongly suggest you research these phenomena so you

can experience firsthand, in a very strong way, what it feels like to hold two opposing views, and how to deal with it. In this way you will see how our current beliefs may not hold any validity in many areas of our lives. If you can free yourself from (or at least understand) belief traps you may also be less guilty of editing out things that may be true, good, right and helpful but in conflict with your current belief structures.

Sand Paper Island

Here is a great metaphor: Let's say there was an isolated island where they used sandpaper for everything—washing their cars, brushing their teeth, showering and cleaning their furniture; they even removed pimples and tattoos with sandpaper! It's their universal cleanup tool and it's all they have ever known or seen. It's all their parents and grandparents knew. It is the only tool they have ever known, or tried, for those types of activities.

On this island there are public figures, news actors, teachers and shamans that continually drum into the populace the many uses and benefits of sandpaper. Based on their experiences, beliefs and current level of thinking, it is a very valuable tool in their society.

Then you arrive with some soft soap. Can you imagine the looks on their faces as you start trying to replace their tough sandpaper with your soft soap? How would all the sandpaper manufacturers react? What would local leaders think of you? What would everyone with large vested interests in the sand paper industry try to do to your reputation, web site and demonstrations? What would they start saying to you and what lies would they spread about you, as you disrupted their sandpaper culture and businesses? I would bet like all new and better information, both the message and messenger would pass through the three stages of truth: First, ridicule. Second, violent opposition. Third, acceptance as self-evident.

Oftentimes we stick with old, outdated practices simply because we are comfortable; it's all we've ever known and it has been—to varying degrees—working for us. When we look back at history we find that many practices and industries are like this island, with its own language, ideological inbreeding and recycling of people, customs and tools. In fact I'm sure that in the future many of our current practices and industries will be seen the same way.

Take a good look at your life, I think we've all been guilty, at one time or another, for sticking with "sandpaper" for too long....

Exercise: Try to identify some of your current sandpaper practices (this is deceptively difficult, because it's nearly impossible for you to identify your current sandpaper because we all think and behave within our current level of thinking!). Of course someone from a different culture or industry could probably make a list of your sandpaper rather quickly! Then you'd have to test their suggestions for a period of time in order to determine which is better. Sometimes we need someone from a different island to change our perspectives. What's important here is the willingness to investigate and analyze our current lives, in a detached way, with the intention of improving ourselves and those around us. Leave no stone unturned.

Scrambled Word

How many times have you seen a person talk too much or a salesperson talk themselves out of a sale? How many times have you done it? I know I have.

Here is a funny sales joke: It's said that Samson killed a thousand men with the jaw bone of an ass, and perhaps as many sales are lost every day by salespeople using the exact same weapon! We talk too much!

Exercise: Rework the word SILENT into another word that has everything to do with the tip in this chapter… hint, it's not tinsel!

We have two ears and one mouth for a reason. The best advice in many situations is to simply shut up and observe.

Selling is a Journey

Most of us are familiar with the term, "Life is a journey, not a destination." It is a reminder that as we move toward our goals, achieving some and missing a few, we should learn from and even enjoy the process as much as the achievements themselves, for this helps us to attain greater fulfillment along the way, no matter the outcomes.

The same holds true of selling. Oftentimes, salespeople are so focused on their best prospects that they forget to cultivate others. Then the jubilation of closing the sale is quickly followed by the realization that they have to go about getting more prospects, and fast!

If you are a salesperson always looking to sell more, you might want to spend less time basking in the glory of your last sale and more time asking yourself how you could have made that last sale easier or more profitable. Mediate on the good and the bad of how you sold it, and move on to getting your next prospect quickly!

Exercise: Immediately after closing a sale, make whatever notes you feel will be important to remember regarding your future contact with your client or the transaction. Then shut your eyes for thirty seconds and ask yourself, "What did I do well and what could I have done better?" as you replay that sale from front to back, organize and put away their file and then immediately take some actions that will help you sell something now or at some time in your future!

Sensitivity Meter

Sometimes the most profound wisdom is also the simplest. As children we learned to say, "Sticks and stones may break my bones but words will never hurt me!" when someone calls us names. But the truth is we often internalize what others say. Remember, words in and of themselves are powerless. Many people don't weigh their words carefully or considerately before they speak but that doesn't mean what they say has to affect you. If you look at many of the tensions in the world you will realize most of them are caused by words alone!

In my opinion, in life and in business, it is very important that we learn how to lead by example and shut off or turn down our sensitivity meters rather than impose our version of the world or "political correctness" (a modern term for a gag order) on everyone else. We cannot control how others will speak to or around us, nor do we have the right to impose our own standards on them. When you are emotionally stirred just by someone else's words, you have given all your power to them.

Remember, it's never the language that's the problem but our reaction to the language, so stop allowing what others simply say to harm you with just words and start owning your own experience and reactions.

But of course you must choose your own words carefully, as there is no guarantee that others around you are trying to develop in this same way. You are the master of your unspoken words, but once spoken they are the master of you!

Sell or be Sold

When I'm at home, at work, at the gym, in yoga, at a soccer game, in a restaurant or at Starbucks (see a pattern of where I spend my time?) every interaction is an opportunity to observe and practice persuasion skills. One of the most important of these skills is creating the "agreement frame."

What is the agreement frame? It's that fantastic combination of an almost imperceptible smile and nod when people are talking. You turn your ear ever so slightly towards them, thereby communicating an interest in them and whatever it is they are expressing. You'll see him or her smile and nod back, mirroring you. What you won't see are the very real biochemical changes in both of you, drastically increasing rapport and good feelings for each other.

Creating an agreement frame puts you well on your way to controlling, creating and maintaining a relationship or a sale. This simple but powerful skill cannot be overstated and must be mastered if you want to become a top communicator or persuader, because whether we realize it or not, in one way or another we are always selling or being sold. This technique will make you instantly better at all your interpersonal connections.

Exercise: For an entire week, practice the art of a small smile, nod and lend an ear and notice the impact it has on others and your interactions with them. You'll find that by improving their attitude, it's much easier to maintain your own!

Sleep on It

Have you ever considered why we use particular words and phrases to describe an experience? For example, we say we are "falling asleep" but we obviously don't really fall anywhere (I for one can't remember the last time I went to bed and fell down). Or what about the term "rising" in the morning? We really don't physically rise when we first wake up because we are still lying down.

While these terms are not literal, they do verbalize what your mind does at the moment of sleep or waking. Your mind has a conscious component that is paying attention to what you're reading right now, and an unconscious component that does not need to pay attention to your breathing, how your foot feels in your left shoe or any ambient noises around you unless your conscious attention is brought to it. Realize it or not, your mind takes in, stores and deletes an avalanche of information all day long.

Sleep plays a critical role in processing and dealing with that avalanche. There's a wise saying: "Never go to bed angry." Why? Because you may wake up angrier. Emotions can "marinate" during the night and by morning are at full potency, whether pleasant or painful.

When you sleep, your conscious mind takes a break and does some housekeeping while your subconscious mind takes over. It continues to regulate all of your bodily functions, triggers you to roll over, and maintains an awareness of your surroundings. There are other important processes going on as well. Sleep studies suggest that new neural pathways are being set as myelin sheathing surrounds brain neurons and dendrites, strengthening relationships with things that you gave attention to that day. This presents us with a fascinating opportunity: we can give "homework" to the subconscious mind while we sleep.

For example, write out a direct statement of how you would like your life to be in the future and read it aloud with emotion as a command in bed before falling asleep. Or take your goals and gratitude's list and review it just before falling asleep. Or, visualize a particular situation and state exactly how you want it to be.

Like everything else in this book, I have practiced and taught this personal development strategy for years, and I can say for a fact that it will effortlessly transform you and your life over time.

Exercise: First write out your bedtime affirmation statement, place it beside your bed and then read it aloud before falling asleep and again upon awakening every day. Second, always sleep with a pen and paper or voice recorder beside your bed, so if you wake up with a great idea or have an impactful dream, you have somewhere to record it before you forget!

Being mindful of what you expose yourself to before you fall asleep, and how you can influence your future by directing your mind just before and after slumber is valuable knowledge, but it must be acted upon.

A few years ago while moving things from one of my homes to another, I was rearranging some books on a shelf when a piece of paper slipped out of one of them and fluttered to the floor. I picked it up and saw it was a bookmark I had created years before. As I read it my mouth dropped and I got chills up my back. It was a direct command sleep assignment I used to read aloud in bed before falling asleep. The reason for my chills was that all of it had come true! In fact, I had surpassed my goals in some areas. As I read those goals I could remember the motivation behind the pains and constraints I felt in many areas of my life at that time; now, I was so far beyond them it almost seemed like someone else's wish list. Truly remarkable. Below is the exact message I had on that bookmark, with some omissions for my privacy:

"Unlimited and infinite abundance guides me. Everyone is free, and it feels great. I am peacefully grateful and enjoy perfect health, wealth, opportunities, energy and love. I am always mindful of my and the world's precious potential. I become smarter, stronger and healthier daily. Earning $_____ without debt and a personal net worth of $_____, I am excited about my future. Improvement is easy as I go inside my mind and become quiet, only focusing on what I can control."

If you are curious about where I was at when I wrote that command, simply write the inversion of each of those statements, and you wouldn't be far off.

Spread the Smiles

Most of us have highly functioning mirror neurons that allow us to look at another human being and have some idea what he/she is feeling. When a person gives you a hostile look, you feel very differently than you do when someone smiles at you. You smile and nod back, and if they seem happy you may begin to feel happy as well. (Just an FYI for you animal lovers: dogs are pack animals and have mirror neurons and cats are loners and do not, which explains a lot about their behavior around us!)

Additionally, seeing a smile or moving your facial muscles into a smile gives your brain signals to release those happy hormones, endorphins. So when you smile at someone you are affecting your biochemistry as well as theirs, in a positive way! The opposite occurs with negative facial expressions, so become aware of yours, for yourself and others around you.

When I was younger I used to get into all sorts of trouble for no apparent reason. Not surprisingly, I also looked the part.

In high school, a detective came to our class. He was looking for young men to stand in as "extras" in criminal line-ups and felt I, an introverted angry punk rocker, had the "right look" and "attitude" for the role. (It makes me laugh just writing that!)

The police station was just down the street from my school, so a couple of times a month I would show up there and

172

play my part, for which I was paid five dollars. Even better, I had gotten the okay from the school principal, which meant I was able to miss even more school than I already did. I would put my clothes and jewelry into a tagged plastic bag and slip on blue coveralls, then get in the lineup with the other "suspects." It was odd, standing there, doing the requisite straight ahead, left and right turn poses knowing the victim of the crime was on the other side of the two-way mirror, trying to discern the guilty party.

My aggressive stature, which had served me well growing up in various circumstances and in sports, was a major hindrance when I first entered the world of customer service and sales. I have what's called "resting bitch face" and if not careful to lighten up, I can instill agitation in those who are in my presence. I quickly realized that in order to be successful I would have to change my habitual expressions and body language so that people reacted to me in a more positive and friendly way.

Here's the really interesting part: I found I was able to increase my customers' feelings of good will just by smiling and having yellow smiley faces on my desk. Sort of like when politicians kiss babies, minus the politician, babies and kissing, if you know what I mean. I was very surprised to find that even inanimate smiles can change someone's state.

Exercise: Go to Google Images and pull up that classic, yellow and black smiley face we all know and love. Print a few in color and place them in your office in strategic locations. You might want to bring a small stuffed animal in your office as well. Studies have also shown that people are more honest and kind when a stuffed animal is nearby.

With these few, simple tips you can create a friendlier workspace, increased receptivity from your buyer and help create an Unstoppable Attitude for yourself and those around you!

Softeners and Builders

By not negatively affecting other people's attitudes it helps keep your attitude positive, as you reduce the negative fall-out and emotional shrapnel of those around you.

Did you know that asking the right questions at the right times is a highly coveted skill? Well, it is—just ask any successful salesperson (or police detective). Along with your tone and body language, proper timing of "public" and "private" questions helps to build rapport with your target and make him/her feel as though you are having a conversation, not conducting an interrogation.

You can also soften your questions by using what I call a "softener." Some examples are lead-ins such as "Just curious…", "By the way…", and "I was wondering…." They soften your questions and make them seem more conversational. For example, instead of asking someone, "What do you do for a living?" try asking, "Just curious, what do you do for a living?" with a soft, perhaps even casual tone.

Once you get someone talking, pay attention. If they reveal something personal in an area of their interest, you want to make use of a "builder." Some examples of builders are "Oh wow!", "You're kidding!", "Cool!", "Neat!" and "Awesome!" Remember, people love to talk about themselves, especially if you seem interested, so be sure you have an enthusiastic tone. It can be effective to establish common ground with people, but that can be hard to do if you don't have anything in common with them and you certainly don't want to lie about what your interests are just to try and connect with someone. So rather than try to find common interests, just chat about their interests and while you do, seem interested! Most people's attitudes improve if they feel others are interested in them, and most people love talking about themselves.

Make use of both softeners and builders and notice the quality and quantity of your conversations improve. If you want to be interesting, you must be interested. Combine this with my previous suggestions—smiling, nodding and lending an ear—and you are well on your way to being perceived as having a very pleasing personality, because like everything else, people's perception is their reality. Sometimes you have to fake it until you make it!

Exercise: Start incorporating softeners and builders into all your verbal and written interactions today.

Summon a Loved One

The type of energy you feel and exude depends on what you choose to focus on. If you spend the day thinking of someone you don't like, the energy or vibe you put out will be completely different than if you think of someone you love or someone that makes you smile or laugh. What causes this effect? Who knows and who cares, just know that it's true!

Exercise: Place the initials, names or pictures of your favorite friends, family, pets, customers and co-workers in your office and glance at them regularly. You will feel an instant boost in your energy and mojo and others will react to you accordingly.

Study It

As I mentioned earlier, the first book I ever finished was the Tony Robbins' self-help masterpiece "Awaken The Giant Within". The book "called to me" and was exactly what I needed at the time. I felt as though I could not put it down.

This was a far cry from the experience I'd had while trying to read books for school. A few pages in and my eyes would become heavy and I found it impossible to stay awake. Funny as it sounds, I actually thought I might have a sleep disorder triggered by reading, even though as far as I knew no such affliction existed. The truth was I had never found a topic I was really interested in.

That all changed when I realized that books could help me improve myself on a personal and professional level and shave years off my growth. Suddenly I was reading every self-help book I could get my hands on. My reading list eventually expanded to those around sales and business, then health and wealth. Today, I am a voracious consumer of books, courses and video content on YouTube. Why the big turnaround? Because I finally found my passion. Put up your hand if you want to be a little healthier, wealthier or happier? I imagine everyone reading this just put up their hand. It seems to be built into our human DNA or spirit.

Which one of those three things do you have a little more of now, health, wealth or happiness? Which one of the three do you pay the most attention to, study the most, spend the most time or money on? Notice any correlation?

Anything worth having is worth studying, spending time and money on. In fact, the mere acts of studying, spending time and money on something increases the odds of you getting more of it.

Why? We only spend our time and money on things that we are interested in and whatever we focus our energies on expands. It's a double feedback loop that builds upon itself over and over. The more you learn the more you earn merits towards it!

How much would I know about you if I had your credit card statement, if I knew where you spent your time and what you read or paid attention to on the Internet?

So, whatever you want more of, study it and spend time and money on!

Exercise: Do a time, money and attention audit on yourself to discover what it reveals about you and where you are headed.

For example, what sort of books are on your bookshelves at home? What do you watch on TV, what websites do you visit, what YouTube channels do you frequent and what radio stations do you listen to? What patterns do you see?

The same goes with where you spend your money and time.

Anything you give attention to will expand.

Success Dress

No matter what you do for a living or what the dress code is, dress with purpose. Choose your work clothes with attention and intention; they should clearly signal to you and the world that you're serious about what you do.

Exercise: Imagine that before you get dressed, you grab a bottle of Teflon spray, whatever color you imagine the spray to be is right for you. Spray every inch of your body, without missing one crease, nook, cranny or bulge. This Teflon coating is impermeable to negativity and rejection, so the rejection and negativity of the world, that would hurt a normal mortal, will now slide right off of an unaffected you.

After picturing yourself dressed for success covered in colored Teflon, affix an imaginary name tag to your shirt that says "Apprentice." This label will remind you to stay humble, open minded and curious throughout your day, so you will be constantly trying to improve.

Lastly, imagine taking a drill about two inches in diameter and drilling it through your head from ear to ear. Now, this may seem to sting a bit, so spray the inside of that hole with your imaginary Teflon spray to create a silky smooth and soothing surface. This hole will let the word "no" slide in one ear and out the other! Intelligent polite persistence eliminates resistance, so being unaffected by rejection is important.

Dressed with attention and intention, wearing your Apprentice name tag, coated in colored Teflon and with a hole in your head, you are now dressed for success! Go get 'em, soldier!

Success Index

Exercise: Hold a goal that you have in mind, and honestly rate yourself in the following three areas from 1 to 10 (1 is bad and 10 is great).

<u>Desire to Learn</u> More About Anything Connected to This Goal _____/10?

<u>Willingness to Change</u> any and all Habits Related to its Attainment _____/10?

<u>Focus to Execute</u> the Daily Tasks Necessary to Move Toward It _____/10?

Take your answers and multiply them by each other. A perfect score is 1000.

For example, if you scored 5 on each, 5x5x5 = 125.

Shift the decimal point one space to the left, and you have 100 for the 1000 score and 12.5 for this example. Then convert to a percentage. So 100 is 100% and 12.5 becomes 12.5%.

This may sound hard to believe, but in my experience, doing this with thousands of professionals, your percentage answer is the odds or probability, that you will hit your goal! I've used this remarkably accurate predictor on myself, business evaluations, athletes, a sports team's odds of winning and even election results!

Imagine you're coaching a team, and you're assessing a player. If this player had a low desire to learn, how much are they actually absorbing at practice? Will it affect their ability to improve? Absolutely. If you're doing what you've always done, you're going to keep getting what you've always gotten. Let's say this person had little willingness to change? Even if they have a high desire to learn, their low willingness to change will hold them back! Let's suppose they had a high desire to learn, a high willingness to change but a lack of focus to execute? They will still stagnate!

Can you see how those three areas are crucial indicators and predictors of how successful any person or group will be, in any endeavor? And how they compound your odds of success or failure when combined with each other?

I strongly suggest you test this formula right now on a few people and organizations you are familiar with to see for yourself how accurate and insightful this can be. You can even make stock picks based on how you rate a company in these areas!

And here is the best part: you have 100% control over each area, and by improving each area, you simultaneously stack the deck in your favor!

SW, SW, SW, N!

Let's face it, not everyone will like us, accept us, agree with us, or buy from us. And because of the law of large numbers, the more you put yourself out there the more rejection you will face! I can tell you from experience that while it's statistically the same to be told no by two out of four people vs. 2000 people out of 4000, those two situations certainly feel different! The point is, when you go for massive success, be prepared for massive rejection!

Here's another tidbit about probability: I believe that about 30% of the people we sell to weren't "sold" by us at all—they decided to buy before they met us and would have bought from anyone that day as long as the sales person didn't screw things up. I also think that 10% of the people we don't sell could never be sold, as they lacked any interest or were determined from the outset not to buy anything from anyone. A few of the people we sell will become close friends and a few of the people we sell we will regret selling, because (and again, this is the law of probability) they might be a wee bit nucking futs!

As for the vast majority in the middle, remember that good people have bad days and bad people have good days, all of which we can affect by our interactions with them. The good news is that when we lose a sale, we have the opportunity to reflect and see where we may have dropped the ball and self-correct for the next time. Onward and upward!

This is not an invitation to obsess over missed opportunities, games lost or shots messed up, as this can become a major emotional, mental, time and energy drain. We can't afford to carry emotional baggage from one day, one person or one sale to the next. We want to replay our victories, learn from our losses and MOVE ON!

We know the best time to sell something is right after you just sold something. You're breathing right, moving well, focused, clear, confident, are giving off a great vibe and have a very recent blueprint of a sale in your mind. The worst time to try to sell something is when you are thinking about the ones you missed. People will respond to you entirely differently when you're carrying negative emotional baggage. The easier you can forget about your past failures and move on quickly, the more successful you will be and avoid the typical ruts so many average performers can get into.

What does SW, SW, SW, N stand for? Some Will (buy from you or like you or whatever), Some Won't, So What, NEXT!

Ten Areas

Being able to find bigger and better meanings in all that I do, and having goals and interests in many different areas has added a lot of spice to my life over the years.

There is no limit to the meanings and purposes you can find in your life, regardless of your interests or profession. I know I've strived to make people proud of me; connect to a higher source; improve my skills and knowledge; prove some people right and others wrong; improve my cash flow and/or pay off debt; acquire great assets; help others develop and succeed; leave a legacy; advance an entire industry; see what emotions / thoughts I can expand or contract; and feel or look better physically.

Exercise: Take out a pen and piece of paper, and write down at least one goal in each of the following areas:

Income	**Debt**
Knowledge	**Skill**
Personal	**Social**
Emotional	**Spiritual**
Physical	**Mental**

I know firsthand that you can become addicted to helping others and to your own personal development. Having several areas to goal-set around are fundamental to the science of achievement and the art of fulfillment, not to mention having some zest in your life every day. And what I have found is that hitting a goal in any area gives you the energy and excitement to start tackling goals in other unrelated areas, which leads to even more momentum and massive changes to come!

For instance, let's say you set a goal of doing fifty push-ups. Each day as you go through your workout, you imagine yourself saying that magic number out loud when you finally do it! When you hit your goal and you know it was due to your change in focus and effort, this will install a belief and confidence to go after another goal, because you now know you can achieve what you set your mind to! Success breeds more successes and momentum creates ever-increasing amounts of personal power!

The Seven Ps

Principles

Practices

Psychology

Process

Patterns

Predictability

Probability

Another way to reduce your chances of failure is to study and master The Seven Ps within your business or personal situation.

Exercise: Here is a basic definition of each area, but try to come up with a list of 3 to 5 things in each category that are in the direction of the changes you wish to make or the success you want to continue...

<u>Principles</u> are laws, rules or standards that can never be broken. What are some standards you will never break?

<u>Practices</u> are strategies or techniques that are necessary to master. What are the top techniques you need to master?

<u>Psychology</u> is to find better ways of thinking and reacting. How can you change your views and habits to improve your progress?

<u>Process</u> is the way or order in which certain behaviors or tasks are executed. What are the key processes and in what areas?

<u>Patterns</u> show up in metrics that help you identify what is and isn't working. What are the most important patterns and metrics of your endeavor that you need to track?

<u>Predictability</u> is one of the major outcomes of mastering the previous 5 Ps. In what areas of your endeavor are you trying to create the most predictability?

<u>Probability</u> of success rises and failure falls if you honor the previous 6Ps. What is the final result you are trying to achieve and what measurable results are you after?

The Gap

Throughout life, we often have gaps between where we are, and where we want to be.

Several years ago, I was fortunate enough to visit the Grand Canyon and it made a profound impact on me. The size and scope of it is hard to explain. At The West Point, there were two towers standing opposite each other, with the vastness of the canyon in between. More than a century ago, the towers were connected with a massive cable that moved mining equipment and workers back and forth across the canyon. The gap between the two towers was roughly one mile across and almost a half-mile deep, and I could only imagine the relief the workers must have felt as they climbed out of the cargo bucket after their hour-long journey across.

It struck me as a great analogy for where we are and where we want to be in life, with a gap between now and our better future selves. And as with anything else, just getting started can be the hardest part of the journey.

So just climb in your bucket and get going!

Thermostats

We are all controlled by some unseen forces I like to call our "Thermostats" or internal settings that dictate why we behave in the way we do, whether positive or negative.

It can be hard to analyze ourselves, so start by thinking of people you work with or those you know well and observe the following behaviors and patterns:

The Money Pattern: How do some commissioned sales people start to behave if they're having an above-average month? Some work harder, while others start coming in late and going home early. How do some people behave during slow times? Some ignore conditions they can't control such as the economy, weather and news and start analyzing and cultivating ways in which they can turn things around, and others blame everything and everybody but themselves for the slide. Some will even contract GIAGOTOSS (Grass is Always Greener on the Other Side Syndrome) and quit, leaving all their current customers behind. They start anew somewhere else, only to find things are pretty much the same over there. How do you behave when your income is more or less than you expected, and who do you blame? What sort of lifestyle have you become accustomed to and how does living much above or below your current level make you feel?

The Time Pattern: Again, with regards to a commissioned sales person or entrepreneur, how long can you go without taking a call, making a call, sending an email, texting a prospect, talking up a suspect, et cetera, before you start to get nervous, upset or anxious? Does this change according to how skinny or fat your pay has been in the recent past? A businessperson with a short time zone is compelled to be busy all the time. How short or long is your time zone?

The Comfort Pattern: How easily and often do you step outside of your habitual behaviors while chasing down a goal? Remember for things to change for you, things have to change about you, so being resistant to doing things in different ways will only have you repeating things that may not be working. How often do you make yourself do things that are uncomfortable to you?

Exercise: With these three considerations, in what areas do you need to work on your internal thermostats the most—your money, time or comfort patterns?

Three Requirements for Growth

In life, there are three things that need to happen before you can make any improvements.

First, you have to recognize what is not working. We all have scotomas (a psychological blind spot) in some areas, not noticing or realizing how certain thoughts or behaviors are affecting our lives. I'm sure you have a friend who repeats the same mistakes over and over again in some area of their life. When you tell them what they are doing wrong, their eyes seem to glaze over, or they push back, oblivious to what they are doing or what you are saying. They literally do not see it and maybe don't want to. If you don't recognize what is not working it is impossible to change. This is why it can be beneficial to approach your personal and professional life with a pair of fresh eyes, whether they are yours or someone else's.

Secondly, once you recognize where you need help and why, you have to modify your thoughts. It's wise to mentally rehearse your new ways of thinking, reacting and acting, so that you can test your modifications before you move to step three in the real world.

Lastly, you need to execute your new thoughts and behaviors until they become a habit and replace whatever it is you were doing before.

And remember, change is certain but improvement is not, so recognize, modify and execute better processes continually. These are the three fundamental steps for growth.

Three Ways to Learn

We only have three ways to learn a skill:

- Experience
- Trial and error
- Modeling

Let's talk briefly talk about all three…

Experience: We all develop experiences along the way, but if you wanted to master a skill or learn how to do something complex, relying solely on your own experiences takes way too long, and will cost you a ton of unnecessary mistakes. Let's say you wanted to learn Mixed Martial Arts (MMA) or how to cook a kick-ass pizza…how many bruises, broken bones and burnt crusts would you experience before you learned more effective and efficient ways?

Trial and Error: While accumulating our experiences, we need to pay attention to what's not working, what is, and to make our adjustments accordingly. But if you aren't the first person to ever do what you are trying to learn, why waste all that effort on the trials and pain on the errors?

Modeling: This is the most effective, efficient, elegant and natural way for us to learn. How did we learn how to walk, talk, eat, cross the road and tie our shoes? We modeled, or copied, the activities of a mentor because we wanted the same results as them. This is exactly how most Eastern teachings work with regard to mastering such things as yoga or martial arts—copy your master. In fact, it's commonplace for the pictures of the teacher's masters to be in their dojo or studio as a humble reminder of the lineage of learning and teaching they are building upon. When you model excellence you are taking advantage of your mentor's years of experience, often turning decades of learning into a couple of years, months, or even days! Humans are natural modelers: monkey see, monkey do. The question is, are you utilizing the best attitudes, skills and habits that will catapult you to the levels of achievement and fulfillment you want in your life? I knew that for me to become more I needed many new blueprints, in many areas, as a reference point. So I started seeking out new peer groups and models at workshops, books, audio courses, professional mentors and historical figures. To model properly, you need to do a few things:

- Drop your ego and realize that you are not perfect and some people are better at certain things than you.

- Be humble and honest with where you are right now; then pick a specific goal and create a plan using your model as a guide.

- Work your plan and track your progress.

- Stop trying to find the perfect person to model. Remember, you aren't modeling the whole person, just their specific traits and skills of your choosing.

- Look for the little differences that might be making the big differences for them. You do this by using your sensory acuity to assess everything they are doing.

100% Effort

When I was 22, the economy entered a brutal recession. The Chrysler dealership where I was working was one of the casualties, so I started repossessing cars for about $1,500 a month while also trying to finish my university degree and running a property maintenance business on the side for extra cash, all in the midst of a bunch of personal issues swirling around me.

I was an occasional smoker back then, and one day while standing outside having a cigarette with my mentor, he made some insightful comments about my lack of effort. "Duane, I can tell you don't like what you are doing for a living and I estimate you are using about 40% of your potential. I hope you know you're creating a situation that will keep you stuck in this job forever." When I asked what he meant, he replied, "There are only three ways up and out of any job:

- Promotion: but your bosses won't want you working with them unless you've been giving it 100%. Remember, you are supposed to make their jobs easier, not harder.

- Headhunted: but no one will want to steal you away from your current job and have you work for them unless they see you are giving it 100%.

- Repeat business and referrals: but no one will give you more business or send you their friends, families and associates unless you gave them 100% and they count on you doing the same for those people they refer to you.

So, Duane, you only get hurt when you don't give it 100%!"

Have you ever had a moment when everything was suddenly clear and logical? Well, this was one of those moments for me—I saw that my choices and lack of effort were trapping me. It was so profound that I can even remember the weather that day! From that day forward I took his 100% message to heart!

Toe to Bum

We all work within, and serve, a community of some type or another. Your industry, for example, is a community in and of itself.

In 1929, Hungarian writer Frigyes Karinthy's wrote about the "six degrees of separation," the theory that everyone on the planet is connected to every other person on the planet through a chain of acquaintances that has no more than five other people. In 1970, Joe Girard had a similar contention—his "Law of 250" stated that most everyone is very closely connected to about 250 people. Because of our connectedness, our reputation is very important. As they say it's not just who knows you, but how they know you, that is crucial. It is even crazier when you realize that both of these concepts were developed before the Internet and social media!

How connected are we now? How much damage could someone do to you on social media if they didn't like your attitude? How fast could someone try to tarnish your reputation, and how widespread could the damage be? Consider our smartphones with their microphones, cameras and screenshots—how much information and what kind of information could someone gather and disperse about you?

For good or bad, the United States has just elected President Trump, who bypassed mainstream media and used social media to connect with voters and have like-minded voters connect with each other! So if you have been slow to realize the massive impact of social media it's time to wake up.

Technology has changed six degrees of separation into something like "one degree of separation," and Joe's "Law of 250" into Duane Marino's "Social Media Law of 25,000". We are all directly connected now and can spread any message far and wide almost instantly.

Decades ago, I heard the adage, "Never step on any toes because one day they may be connected to the same bum you will have to kiss!" and was struck by the truth of it. Today, more than ever, we have to be careful about what we say, what we do, what we "like" on-line, what we post and to whom.

We all make mistakes and not everyone will like us. But don't go around making enemies or stepping on toes; maintain your reputation and character like your life depends on it, because in many ways it does.

Exercise: Honestly ask yourself if you've ever intentionally stepped on any toes, how and with whom. Then clear your subconscious mind and negative consequences (karma) by calling or messaging them, and turn yourself in. Don't expect or want anything from them such as forgiveness or understanding. Just do it so you can move fully past it.

Natural and Unnatural Fears

They say we start and end our lives with two natural fears: the fear of loud noises and the fear of falling. These fears keep us out of harm's way when we are vulnerable.

We also have two unnatural fears that are socialized into us: the fear of not being liked or loved and the fear of not being enough. Think about it: how many times in your life have people told you to sit down, shut up, looked at you with disapproval, laughed at you, reminded you of failures, threatened to tattle on you, et cetera?

There have been studies done on how you can use these ingrained fears on individuals, institutions and organizations that you seek to control, discredit or attack. Think of the terms "quack", "conspiracy theorist", "truther", et cetera, all of which were designed to embarrass anyone that even talked about certain topics and make most people just look the other way. The fear of embarrassment and rejection are a powerful control mechanism and our handlers know it.

How many things in life have you not done or attempted to do because you were afraid of embarrassment, failure or being inadequate? If you're "normal" you probably couldn't even begin to count them. How much growth and joy have we denied ourselves because of these fears?

Earlier in the book I mentioned sayings such as "FEAR stands for False Evidence Appearing Real" and "a coward dies a thousand deaths but a warrior only dies once!" And I think they are worth repeating. These sayings may be cliché, but they are also very true.

I have found that the awareness of these natural and unnatural fears has helped me convince myself into tackling many things I may have otherwise steered away from.

Exercise: Write down a few things you are not doing because of either the fear of not being liked or loved and the fear of not being enough. Now look at your goals, and ask yourself if you are not applying full effort on some of them because of the fear of not being liked or loved or being enough…?

Duane Marino Version 49.11

As I sit here and write this chapter, I remind myself I am Duane Marino Version 49.11.

If I was a piece of software, being 49 years and 11 months old, I am really just a current version of my ever-changing self. In a few months every cell in my body will have turned over and been replaced, even my bone tissue. I hope to get older, but that's no excuse to become irrelevant or stale.

What is a software company supposed to do with their programs? Update and improve them regularly! If they don't, the marketplace will decide they are stale and irrelevant and they will be out of business!

Did you know Blackberry fathered and at one time dominated the smartphone industry? For years they were the standard and benchmark for excellence. Now you say their name and people chuckle because they are seen as archaic and have just recently announced they are exiting the smartphone business entirely. What was their mistake? I believe it was twofold: they became sluggish and lazy due to enormous successes and had a scotoma (or blind spot) for the market demand of apps. They stand as a lesson that anyone can be pushed into obscurity, no one is too big to fail and that unless you evolve you most certainly will dissolve!

I can tell you with absolute certainty that Duane Marino Version 49.11 is different and in many ways better than Duane Marino Version 48.11. I consider myself a work in progress and am always looking for my next edge in some area of my life.

How old are you today? What version of you is reading this chapter? How have you changed over the past few months and years? In what ways can you work on yourself as you seek your next best you?

As I have said a couple times, change is certain but progress is not. If you see yourself as your main competition, in what ways can you compete with who you were yesterday, and make your future self a little better, stronger, wiser, more effective or efficient? This can be an exhilarating and fun way to live, because every day becomes another exciting opportunity to grow and evolve.

Wake up Your Senses

Exercise: Here is a very cool Martial Arts exercise that will help you experience your surroundings and life more fully:

- Sit straight up with your hands on your lap and look straight ahead

- Fix your eyes on one spot in front of you, and then work on increasing your peripheral vision as wide as possible, taking in all the colors and textures, noticing everything in your area of sight with equal weight and attention until you can see in a full 180 degrees without moving your eyes to the left or the right...

- Now start to listen to all the sounds, of all volumes and tones, that are happening around you, above you, below you...

- Scan slowly from your toes to the top of your head and feel everything on every inch of your body that you were not noticing a moment ago...

- Move your tongue in your mouth and feel all the textures and tastes that are available to you...

- Take a deep inhalation, feel the air enter your nose, move along your passage ways, strike the back of your throat, move down into your lungs and notice the smells you were not noticing a moment ago...

- **How many things did you notice that you were previously ignoring?**

In order to maintain our sanity and some level of concentration our brain deletes and generalizes the vast majority of the stimulus around us. In doing so, we can become numb and ignorant to the amazing amount of beauty and information that continually surrounds us.

Like all the strategies in this book, I will do this exercise periodically and randomly through the week to make sure I am living fully and appreciating this incredible world we choose to live in!

What a great exercise to demonstrate that your energy truly flows where your focus goes!

And because your mind can only give full attention to one thought at a time, this is an outstanding "active meditation" to do whenever you are feeling stressed, overwhelmed or if you just want to briefly remove yourself from a situation for a few moments. Where your body is, and your mind is, are both fully under your control, and need not occupy the same time or space, unless you want them to.

Cultivate and Analyze Daily

For this final chapter I want to share two meditations I do every single day that help me enormously with my Unstoppable Attitude.

As mentioned earlier, I have mastered a relaxation meditation practice called Transcendental Meditation (TM), and I highly recommend it. With my crazy schedule and constant extensive traveling for over two and a half decades, I am often asked how I've stayed relatively youthful, rested, rejuvenated, fit and keep my energy levels so high, and I give much of the credit to TM, as well as the lifestyle and nutrition suggestions I will make in a few pages.

Also, for about five minutes each day, either while walking or with my eyes closed, I cultivate and analyze my entire life through this series of questions and direct statements I have memorized:

I take a deep breath and say, "I open my mind, intuition and heart to this projection...

1. With humble and deep gratitude, I emotionally recall some impactful experiences, influential learnings and powerful mentors who I have learned from in many areas of my life.

2. How can I do less harm to all sentient beings?

3. My mind is developing on a never-ending continuum, so I will develop it in any way I can, every day.

4. While breathing deeply and incanting, "Thank you!" I think of things I'm grateful for with feeling.

5. How can I be more aligned to give and get unconditional love, passion, infinity, structure, strength and wisdom?

6. While deeply breathing and incanting "I am **THAT** I am," I review my goals and project the energy of that phrase onto each of them.

7. As craving, clinging and ignorance are the causes of all suffering, am I feeling any of them right now and if so in what areas and why?

8. With regard to any decisions I am torn about right now, what does my head, heart and gut say and what is the potential Middle Way?

9. What positive personal and professional traits do I want to maximize?

10. What negative personal and professional traits do I need to minimize?

11. I project compassion, patience, wisdom and tolerance on anyone that may be disturbing me right now.

12. I review my thoughts and behaviors through the lenses of right intentions, right views, right speech, right livelihood, right actions, right mindfulness, right concentrations and right effort.

13. How do I want today to be?

14. What do I have to do today?

15. How am I doing with all my interactions?

16. How do I want this evening to be?

17. Two things I did well yesterday and two things I could have done better?

18. How can I be of more benefit to all sentient beings?

19. Am I living all of these principles to my fullest potential?"

I then take another deep breath and say, "I close my mind, intuition and heart to this reflection...."

"Successful people ask better questions, so they get better answers, and results!"

—*Tony Robbins*

Question: about how long would it take you to do a daily five-minute review of your achievement and fulfillment blueprint? Probably about five minutes a day!

Remember, quality questions create a quality day; quality days create quality weeks; quality weeks create quality months; quality months create quality years; quality years create quality decades; and quality decades create a quality life, and a quality life creates a quality consciousness!

If you're seeking other resources to help you unlock your Unstoppable Attitude efficiently and effectively, in addition to my workshops, books and online resources, I have had many personal positive experiences with the following resources and modalities:

- Tony Robbins traveling "Unleash The Power Within Seminars" as well as his entire Mastery University

- The Monroe Institute's Consciousness Research Workshops in Faber, Virginia

- Tom Campbell's lectures on Consciousness

- The Dalai Lama's Speaking Tour at the University of Hamburg, Germany

- Time Line Regression and Hypnotherapy Sessions and Training with Georgina Cannon through York University in Toronto

- Neurolinguistic Programming Trainings and Interventions with Dr. Wil Horton in Venice, Florida; Richard Bandler in London, England; John Grinder in Murcia, Spain

- Emotional Freedom Technique Sessions with Gary Craig

- A Transformation Vacation that incorporates the ancient plant medicine Ayahuasca at Rythmia Resort in Guanacaste, Costa Rica.

- Applied Kinesiology trainings

- Access Consciousness trainings

If you got this far I want to thank you for finishing my book, playing hard, keeping an open mind and remaining skeptical as you worked through the exercises and readings! I hope the exercises and information in this book helps you as much as they have helped me over the years, along with thousands of others.

My light salutes your light and I wish you all the health, wealth and happiness that you are capable of and destined to become, now and forever!

Until we meet again....

BONUS: UNSTOPPABLE VIBRANCY!

Reader, like everything else, there are factors within our control and outside of it and our health and vitality are no different. So to focus on the things that we have some control over just makes sense. As a realist I recognize that we seem to be programmed to expire around 80 years of age, plus or minus 5 years, no matter what we do. So my goal is to live a high quality and vital life and die a peaceful natural death in old age.

I travel a lot which makes nutritious meal planning very difficult. I am certainly not as disciplined as I should be—I enjoy McDonald's once in a while and even partake in the occasional cigar, cigarette and alcoholic drink. That said I do follow a very healthy lifestyle roadmap most of the time and I want to share it with you. Remember, having an Unstoppable Attitude starts with building your base—your health!

I believe the three fundamental causes of ill health in our modern society are **toxicity, deficiency and the frequency of calories** we consume. When you are researching and applying the following suggestions, keep that in mind. Today, we have a multitude of entirely new causes of toxicity; much of our food is nutritionally deficient, calories come in many forms and are within easy access all the time.

I had mentioned earlier in my book to "follow the money" whenever you are trying to understand many of our modern problems and this is especially true when it comes to much of our food and "sick care" industries. So being part of any real change means to please remember to **"vote with your dollar"** and make very conscious choices about what companies and products will get your votes when you are spending your money! Let's force the market place into giving us bigger and better health choices by making the conglomerates that run the world follow our money!

Vibrant Health Challenge—You be the Judge!

The following information is by no means exhaustive. Use it as an introduction to research some of the things you should try to move away from and why, and those you should move toward. Read just a few minutes each day about health principles and practices from independent resource email newsletters and remember that anything worth having is worth studying.

Do your own research on Google, Bing, Yahoo, YouTube and anywhere else you can get information (as mentioned earlier please know that every major search engine uses different algorithms to pull up or hide searches based on the biases and agendas of the money behind them, so vary your search engines). Be aware that there are many things changing in our environment, with legislation, food industry practices and even how search engines will suppress or "memory hole" inconvenient facts that may hurt certain industries, so be diligent and thorough in your research.

Then begin replacing bad habits with good ones. Even small things can result in big improvements, so START WITH ONE THING AND GO FROM THERE! Don't get caught up with thinking you need to do it all, all of the time. But great health does start with being aware of healthy choices. The information below is designed to act as a catalyst for your research—a menu of choices—not as a program to be followed in its entirety.

Learn how to support your digestive, respiratory, circulatory, musculoskeletal, nervous, energetic, endocrine, lymphatic, hormonal and immune systems. Open the cleansing channels—P.U.R.D. your system: Perspirate, Urinate, Respirate and Defecate daily! Healthy Cells = Healthy Body!

Address cellular toxicity, acidity/alkalinity, insulin, colon health, nutrition, glucose, inflammation, hormones and oxygen to renew cellular health, restore wellness, increase strength and maximize your energy!

Take responsibility for your health and always do your own research. Consult your physician and natural doctor. AN OUNCE OF PREVENTION IS WORTH A POUND OF CURE. COPY THIS AND PLACE IT ON YOUR FRIDGE AND GLANCE AT IT DAILY!

DOs

Detox!

Do deep diaphragmatic breaths several times a day using a 16-hold in / 8-out count; take nature walks; buy a water filter for your shower head or entire home; put nothing on your skin you wouldn't eat, use mineral salt deodorant, natural soap, shampoo, toothpaste, organic coconut oil for skin cream, natural make-up and hair dye; avoid touching thermal receipts such as those from cash registers and avoid plastic containers as they are estrogen mimickers; avoid using a microwave oven; natural home cleaning products; remove mercury dental amalgams by a dentist qualified to do so and replace with porcelain or ceramic and avoid or eliminate root canals; commit to a "digital detox" for a few hours a day or one day a week—this means NO cell phone, computer, TV, iPad, radio, et cetera.

Physical Conditioning!

Two to three times per week minimum: Burst, weight training, Crossfit style or HIIT workouts; skipping; have sex frequently; core work; stretching; rebounding/bouncing; walking; barefoot grounding; yoga; break a sweat every day.

Eat to Live Don't Live to Eat!

Juice fresh vegetables with a slow speed masticating juicer; raw or low heat-cooked fresh (organic) vegetables and cruciferous vegetables and fruits; drink filtered water; (organic) small amounts of gluten free or whole cereals, ancient grains bread, brown rice, potatoes, steel cut oats and kamut pasta; spices and herbs, beans, legumes, nuts, sprouts, dark green/colorful vegetables, seeds, grains; once per week wild seafood and fish from varied sources (as of this writing eat seafood from the Atlantic Ocean—not the Pacific Ocean due to the ongoing radioactive disaster in Fukushima, Japan); locally raised grass-fed organic meat and free run chicken; a salad with every meal using lemon juice or apple cider vinegar instead of normal vinegar; fermented vegetables and drinks; only olive oil, flax and fish oils; cook with avocado or coconut oil.

Start your daily food intake with a handful of nuts and a tablespoon of coconut oil; drink 500ml of filtered water (Kangen Water Filters are world class) or sparkling mineral water for every fifty pounds of body weight with chlorophyll or fresh lemon added; enjoy your food; chew well; eat slowly until full; drink a glass of cold water with a teaspoon of apple cider vinegar ten minutes before your primary meal; limit drinking fluids while eating; most foods and meals should be water-based not oil based; drink green or black tea daily with fresh lemon quarters.

A Peaceful Mind!

Do what brings you joy; avoid negative people / media; do random acts of kindness; each morning spend some time in quiet reflection of gratitudes and goals, planning your day, or meditating/praying; say grace before meals; read motivational/inspirational/educational books before bed.

Support Yourself!

Take a twenty-minute nap each day; finish your hot showers with 3 to 5 minutes of ice cold water; learn and do TM; be in bed by 10pm and up by 5am, sleep in total darkness and silence with a sleep mask and ear plugs if needed; get a moderate amount of sun each day; get a massage; see an Osteopath; infrared sauna and regular gravity fed colon hydrotherapy; shorten your eating window to as few hours as possible eating very well but within only a few hours; listen to uplifting music and laugh all day; drink a glass of sparkling mineral water before bed with a quarter teaspoon of baking soda or a small glass of kombucha!

DON'Ts

Dead Foods!

Reduce/eliminate alcohol, gluten, sugar and caffeine; all electrically dead food and food-like items in cans, boxes, bags, fried, bbq'd, all GMOs , soy, pharmaceuticals, pesticides, frozen, factory foods, MSGs, additives, sweeteners, labels you can't easily understand; processed and natural sugars from any sources; soda pop; commercial fruit juices; avoid fructose and sugar. Ask yourself questions such as, "Would my great-grandmother recognize my food?" and "Earth to Mouth! Does this food go through the fewest steps possible from earth to mouth?" Never eat fruit right after meals, only before, and avoid food for two to three hours before bed.

Processed Fats!

Reduce/eliminate unnatural fats (canola, trans and vegetable.) Ask, "Will this cleanse me or clog me?"

Animal Flesh!

Reduce/eliminate commercial factory farmed fish, factory farmed red meat (prions, nitrates, fear adrenaline, feces, urine, hormones, antibiotics, estrogenic, environmentally terrible, acidic) and factory farmed chicken and move towards wild or free range grass fed. Ask, "Where do cows get their protein from?" (Plants.)

Dairy Products!

Reduce/eliminate all forms of dairy (MAP bacteria, mucous, hormones, antibiotics, difficult protein, acidic). Ask, "Where do cows get their calcium from?" (Plants.)

Balance PH!

Reduce/eliminate addictive and acidic poisons of sugar, salt, vinegar, nicotine, alcohol, caffeine (except for organic black coffee, green and black tea), drugs and vaccines. When using your cell phone keep it a safe distance from body, avoid electronics and Wi-Fi as much as possible and get a Himalayan Salt Lamp to place near your Wi-Fi emitter.

Health-Forming Daily Habits

Drink a glass of hot, filtered water with fresh squeezed lemon immediately upon waking; have a cup of matcha green tea, black tea or black coffee. Enjoy prunes, figs, macadamia and brazil nuts, almonds, walnuts, pumpkin and sunflower seeds. Ten minutes of bouncing on a rebounder; ten minutes of oral oil pulling/sloshing using organic coconut oil after flossing your teeth and before brushing them with natural toothpaste and baking soda; body horse hair brush all limbs and torso towards the heart, snack on fresh vegetables or fruit, eat with nutrition in mind and exercise for 10-60 min daily. Get a good nights sleep with a twenty-minute midday nap or TM, remember to breathe deep, avoid negativity and laugh! Before bed have an occasional chamomile tea or 0.2mg of melatonin. Micro dose cannabis oil.

Duane's Daily Power Smoothie: blend coconut water or coconut milk, tsp. of collagen, tsp. of aloe vera gel, six raw apricot seeds, one tablespoon organic coconut oil, three tablespoons of kefir, one or two whole raw free run organic eggs, a handful of berries, one banana, two tablespoons of New Zealand grass fed whey powder, full tablespoon of Spirulina, full teaspoon chlorella, half a teaspoon bee pollen, one tablespoon chia seeds, two tablespoons raw unpasteurized honey, dropper of fulvic acid minerals, 30 oxy-e drops, dropper of liquid zeolite, tablespoon of Udos oil, one drop of oregano oil, half a teaspoon of turmeric, 1/8 teaspoon of maca root powder, a pinch of ground black peppercorns and 1 teaspoon of pure cinnamon.

Daily supplements: probiotic, liquid vitamin D3, fibre, liver milk thistle, resveratrol, krill oil, digestive enzyme, msm, vitamin K2, CoQ10 ubiquinol, bromelain, kyolic garlic.

Male Support Supplements: (FYI—whether you are male or female, you need to be aware of the thousands of untested chemicals we are exposed to from as early as the womb, which are causing what has been nicknamed "Environmental Castration." Most men are not low in testosterone. They are low in progesterone and high in estrogen and insulin due to the man-made estrogen mimickers in our environment as well as the constant consumption of calories and increasing body fat.) Niacin, Zinc, Magnesium, Selenium, L-Arginine, L-Citruline, DHEA, DIM, Tribulus, Korean Red Ginseng, Gingko Biloba, B Vitamin Complex, Vitamin E, Stinging Nettle, Pycnogenol, D-Aspartic Acid, Boron, Choline, Saw Palmetto, Lycopene, Fenugreek and Ashwagandha. Eat celery, button mushrooms and broccoli to flush out estrogen.

Intermittent fasting (IF) also known as Time-Restricted Feeding (TRF), which I have coined into the phrase:

- **Leasting:** hydration with complete calorie restriction.

- **Beasting:** physical exertion and exercise.
- **Feasting:** compressing your full day's nutrition into just 4 to 8 hours.

This has been one of the best things I have ever implemented. I swear by it on so many levels, I cannot do it justice here. Like everything else in this book, do your own research. There seems to be a lot of misinformation regarding healthful eating that goes against what and when our ancestors ate. Ideally about ½ to ⅔ of your diet should be from healthy fats, with the remaining portion being carbohydrates from vegetables and grains, some fruit and moderate amounts of varied proteins with little to no processed foods. Studies show time restricted feeding causes autophagy and mitophagy, benefits your immune system, mitochondria, brain health and cognitive function, reduces inflammation and free radicals, kills cancer cells, normalizes hormones and slows aging! It is NOT a diet so if you love to eat like I do this is for you! You also must be careful to NOT reduce your overall nutrition or total calories when doing it. Start off by striving to consume calories within only a 12 hour window, then work on reducing that time frame over a period of weeks or months to only a 6 to 4 hour eating window. Monday to Friday, this is my eating pattern and the time of day I choose to eat those calories varies. I typically start my feeding window with a scoop of coconut oil and large handful of nuts and figs, along with my Daily Power Smoothie and supplements as described above. I am off the time restricted program on weekends and eat whenever I want. It will take some time for your body to adapt from burning sugar to burning fat so start slow. Ensure you consume a full day of nutrition, supplements and calories in your feeding window! The shorter the eating time frame (or food celebration as I call it) the better. Outside your eating window consume only black coffee, water and tea. When you consume even one calorie from any source (just chewing gum or eating a nut) insulin is released and then a cascade of other hormonal things start to happen if you are constantly taking in calories through the day. The mental and physical benefits of IF or TRF are astounding. The best part is that it's not a diet and you can literally consume whatever you want within your eating window, and again the shorter the eating window time the better. Do you own research on this. Herschel Walker (mid 50's athlete extraordinaire) has been on a program called One Meal A Day (OMAD) since he was in his 20's, and Dr. Eric Berg and Dr. Mercola have extensive information you may enjoy in books and on the Internet. I know one size doesn't fit all, but please check it out. This combined with finishing my hot showers with 5 minutes of ice cold water has been incredible!

Stomach BONUS: Do you know anyone with either Colitis, IBS or Crohn's? Chances are you do, and if you don't it's because the people you know with these issues are very good at hiding it. These conditions, like many others, have reached epidemic levels today, but were virtually unheard of just a few decades ago. So what's changed? I have several family members and friends who have struggled with these challenges. One in particular almost died from Crohn's, only to go into complete remission for years now (knock on wood) using the information below. Again, this is a guide for your independent research and always follow the money when looking for the answers to any broken system! Google, Bing and Yahoo search "MAP bacteria, Cattle Yohns disease and Human Crohn's disease" and "how pesticides kill insects by causing their guts to leak." Move immediately away from ALL cattle products or dairy of any kind including meat, cheese, yogurt and milk; occasional chicken and fish is okay. Strive for only organic fruits and vegetables that you prepare yourself. Chew your food really well and thoroughly, as digestion starts there. Several tablespoons of coconut oil through the day. Make a daily shake with coconut milk, spirulina, chlorella, aloe gel, banana, raw honey, cinnamon and turmeric. Buy a slow speed masticating juice press and make two carrot and green apple juices daily. Supplement with boswelia, golden seal, bromelain, digestive enzymes, double up on probiotics and drink a small glass of Kombucha. Eat within an eight-hour window daily and avoid gluten. And get plenty of sleep and do relaxation breathing.

Remember, when you feel great, everything is better and easier!

About the Author

Duane Marino is an independent entrepreneur and strategist. As we all strive for continuous improvement, his passion is helping people with maximization of their potential.

Duane believes this is accomplished by exercising honest reflection while moving towards new goals and never letting fear, bad habits, or complacency slow one's progress.

Duane's overall goal is to always leave things better than the way he found them through certain maxims, perspectives, and ways of interaction that include, in part, the following:

- Life and business require that we make contact with others during the regular course of each day. In this small world, every point of contact must have a clear and straightforward intention with outcomes as positive as possible.

- You must be careful not to let your strengths become weaknesses.

- Often, the qualities that contribute to initial greatness are the same ones that lead to eventual failure.

Self-awareness is everything. Without exception, Duane has personally experienced, applied and executed all of the information he teaches.

Unstoppable Attitude is the second sequel to Duane's #1 best-seller, *The Six Sales Powers to Unstoppable Selling*—ISBN: 978-1942389040, Prominent Books, LLC.

Duane lives by the principles, practices, psychology and patterns of all three books.

For more information on Mr. Marino's coaching, feel free to contact him at: www.DuaneMarino.com, or email: info@DuaneMarino.com.

Index